Being of Sound Mind

A book of eccentric wills

By the same author
HOMELANDS OF THE CLANS

Being of Sound Mind

A book of eccentric wills
GERALD WARNER

Illustrations by
Albert Rusling

Elm Tree Books London

First published in Great Britain 1980
by Elm Tree Books/Hamish Hamilton Ltd.
Garden House 57-59 Long Acre London WC2E 9JZ

British Library Cataloguing in Publication Data

Being of sound mind.
1. Wills — Anecdotes, facetiae, satire, etc.
   I. Warner, Gerald
929'.3'09   K820
ISBN 0-241-10471-8

Typeset by Pioneer
Printed in Great Britain by
Redwood Burn Ltd., Trowbridge and Esher.

To my brother,
MICHAEL WARNER

The author and publishers are grateful to Hilary Macaskill and Paul Dacre for the information gleaned from their articles published respectively in the *Guardian,* 10 July 1979, and the *Daily Mail,* 4 December 1979.

Contents

Glossary

CODICIL: supplement or postscript added to a will.

DOCTORS' COMMONS: before the setting up of the Divorce Court and Probate Court in 1857, this was the college of the doctors of civil law in London, which contained a wills' registry.

EXECUTOR/EXECUTRIX: a man or woman appointed to carry out the provisions of a will.

HOLOGRAPH: a will whose entire text is in the handwriting of the testator.

INTESTATE: the term applied to anyone who dies without having made a valid will; this situation is known as *intestacy*.

PROBATE: the legal process by which the validity of a will is established; a will thus authenticated is said to be *proved*.

TESTATOR/TESTATRIX: a man or woman who makes a will.

History of Wills

e brought nothing into this world, and it is certain we can carry nothing out.' So the Church of England, in its burial service, admonishes the faithful to let go their grasp on the accumulated loot of a lifetime. But death does not extinguish the pride of possession, even among Christians. If we can't take it with us, the popular consensus runs, then we can at least make sure that the property we reluctantly leave behind is disposed of in accordance with our precise wishes — however unreasonable, ludicrous, or malevolent these may be. As William Hazlitt expressed it: 'This last act of our lives seldom belies the former tenor of them, for stupidity, caprice, and unmeaning spite.'

It is fitting that the instrument by which a man allocates his possessions after death is called his *will*. For that is exactly what the document is: a public declaration of his arbitrary intentions, perhaps of his extravagant whimsy. A will is the last opportunity for the deceased to impose his wishes on others, either to make an orderly and just distribution of his property, or to settle old scores, or commit a final act of irresponsibility.

What is a last will and testament? The double terminology is not redundant since, strictly speaking, the will originally dealt with landed property, the testament with personal effects. Early wills, of course, were oral.

The first individual reputed to have made his will was Noah — truly an historic occasion, since this was not only the earliest will, but also the largest estate ever recorded! Noah divided the world among his three sons, and St Philaster, Bishop of Brescia, writing in the fourth century A.D., denounced as heretical anyone who

11

disputed this division. (He also anathematised all those who erroneously maintained that the stars remained permanently fixed in the sky, instead of being set in place by God every evening.) Another Old Testament will-maker, Jacob, bequeathed to Joseph 'one portion above thy brethren, which I took out of the hand of the Amorite with my sword and with my bow'. (Genesis, xLviii, 22)

Some historians have maintained that written wills originated with the ancient Egyptians, and knowing their propensity to scribble a hieroglyphic on the slightest excuse, this seems quite likely. It has also been claimed that some scholars were once privileged to find the will of Sennacherib (he who came down like a wolf on the fold, only to get his come-uppance equally promptly) in the Assyrian royal library at Nineveh. Such precious antiquarianism, however, smacks of pedantry; for present purposes it will be sufficient to start with the classical Greeks.

Solon is credited with the introduction of wills into Athens, around 574 B.C. Plato, in 348 B.C., left two farms and four slaves to his son, Adimantes, 'to whom I bequeath also all my chattels as specified in an inventory held and possessed by Demetrius'. A quarter of a century later, his fellow-philosopher, Aristotle, also made his will, in which he was particularly concerned to arrange for the disposal of the female members of his household. 'As soon as my daughter shall be marriageable she is to be given to Nicanor,' he directed; his executors were also to superintend the marriage of his mistress, Herpyllis, and 'see that she does not marry anyone below my condition'.

With even the decadent Greeks organizing themselves sufficiently to bestow their worldly goods, it was not to be expected that a practical and hard-headed race like the Romans would neglect this important area of law. Wills were introduced at Rome by the legal code known as the

Twelve Tables. Sometimes a testator wrote his will in his own handwriting; this was known as *holographum,* and to this day a handwritten will is known as a holograph.

Among notable Roman wills, that of Virgil, in 10 B.C., originally contained a disastrous clause — he ordered the manuscript of the *Aeneid* to be burned. His executors, however, warned him that the Emperor Augustus would never permit this act of philistinism, so Virgil relented and substituted instructions that nobody was to presume to revise the uncorrected verses.

The Divine Augustus himself, when he made his will in 13 A.D., took a firm line with the disorderly women of his family: he forbade the ashes of his daughter and granddaughter — both called Julia and both notoriously promiscuous — to be placed in the sacred tomb of the Caesars when they died.

From these beginnings, wills have never looked back. They have spread throughout all continents and most cultures, growing ever more elaborate, ever more contentious. The Anglo-Saxons, who were a careful people, made three copies of their wills, each matching its neighbour like a tally, and each copy was kept by a different person. This cautious practice lingered on as late as the sixteenth century, when Sir Maurice Berkeley, before going overseas, was said to have left copies of his will in the hands of three friends.

In the Dark Ages, wills were sometimes written on wood.

In the Dark Ages, wills were sometimes written on wood or bark (and even in the twentieth century, as the succeeding pages will show, they have been inscribed on stranger surfaces), but parchment or paper has been the preferred medium of the majority of testators. By common law in England, until the reign of Henry II, a man could dispose at will of only the lesser part of his property; he had to provide for his wife and heirs out of the bulk of his estate.

Early wills give an interesting insight into the domestic economy and social attitudes of the times. A will of 1506 announced that 'I, Alice Love, the wife of Gyles Love of Rye, by the speciall license of my said husband, asked and opteyned' (clearly women's liberation was not a significant force in those days), 'bequeith my para-pharnalle . . . Item, to my suster Mercy my best violet gowne furred with shanks . . . Item to Thomas Oxenbridge my best gilt gyrdell . . .'

Another will of the same period illustrates the perennial desire to hand down heirlooms. Squire John Turvyle, of Newhall, Leicestershire, left to William, his son and heir, 'a bason and an ewer of silver, warnyng and chargyng him, on my blessyng, and as he will answere afore God at the day of dome, that he shall bequeith them after his decesse to his son and heire apparant, and so under this maner and condicion the forsayd basyn and ewer of silver to go from heire to heire while the world endureth'. A more arresting item, in the inventory of goods left by Christopher Smythe, a canon of Durham Cathedral, in 1603, was 'A mapp of the Prodigall sonne, in a fraime, and other two little framed mappes', valued at 3s 4d.

℟oyal wills, of course, attracted the greatest interest. That of Edward I has not survived, but according to the chronicler Froissart, he gave orders for his body to be boiled down and his bones extracted; thereafter, they were to be carried into battle every time an English army marched against the Scots. It is a pity that these instructions were never carried out: a modern interpretation of them would surely give a terrific boost to the morale of the England XV during international rugby matches at Twickenham or Murrayfield, if they were to play with a skeleton supporter in the royal box!

A different colonial problem — the rebellious Irish — harassed Richard II. Before setting out to subdue Ireland in 1399, he made his will. Written in Latin by a clerk, but signed '+ le Roy', it provided for the completion of the nave of Westminster Abbey. A century later, Henry VII's will similarly gave detailed instructions regarding the decoration of his chapel and the ornamentation of his tomb with effigies 'of copure and gilt', but forbade his funeral to be conducted with 'dampnable pompe and oteragious superfluities'.

Some royal wills, however, were destined to be frustrated, as their authors had been throughout their lives. Take, for example, the case of Mr W. R. Smee. Mr Smee was a very talented nineteenth-century administrator, who was called in by the Post Office to reorganize several departments which had fallen into chaos. (Would that his reforms had been more enduring!) His pamphlet on the topical question *Repeal of the Malt Duties* was so impressive that he was consulted by the government on this thorny problem. For twenty years he contributed articles to a variety of newspapers, earning wide respect as a commentator on topics of serious public interest. He was, in short, a typical Victorian polymath, with the energy and breadth of information which distinguished that formidable breed.

That, at any rate, was the workaday Mr Smee. There was, however, another side to this oracle of the malt tax; in his spare time, Mr Smee was pretender to the throne of Great Britain. In 1859, he sent a petition to Queen Victoria, setting forth the grounds on which he believed himself to be the son of George IV. He explained that, as a child, he had been out with his nurse one day, when people recognized him as the Prince of Wales, whereupon a cheering crowd escorted him home. He also remembered being dandled on the knee of George IV, who had said to him, 'Poor boy, poor boy, get on with your learning. A great destiny is preparing for you, though you do not know it.' (This, of course, may simply have been a prediction of Mr Smee's eventual vocation to reorganize the Post Office.)

But not all of his memories were pleasant. Every morning he had been dosed with drugs to induce amnesia; the Duke of Wellington, disguised as a workman, had stalked him round Finsbury Circus. Altogether, he had been subjected to a persecution under which a lesser spirit than his must have wilted. His nominal father, the elder Mr Smee, was alleged to have said of him, in phraseology which might almost have been put into his mouth by Dickens: 'Extraordinary and unheard-of means have been adopted to keep him down, or he must have come to the throne.'

As was to be expected, when Mr Smee came to make his will, he was anxious to advertise his royal origins for the last time by some suitable gesture. So, as a mark of filial piety, he bequeathed his property to the Corporation of Brighton, the seaside resort which owed its fashionable popularity to George IV. The town, without faltering in its loyalty to Queen Victoria, would have been quite happy to accept this gift when the will was published in 1880, but it was contested on the grounds that the testator had suffered from insane delusions. Against this, it was argued that Mr Smee had been an able administrator and a respected and prolific writer on intricate topics, all of which must have been beyond his capacities had he been insane. The judge, nevertheless, overruled the will, declaring that: 'The fact that a man was capable of transacting business, to whatever extent that might go, however complicated the business might be, and however considerable the powers of intellect it might require, did not exclude the idea of his being of unsound mind.'

Apart from royalty, other distinguished people took pains over their wills. In the Middle Ages, they were often more concerned with their spiritual welfare than their earthly goods. Such concern came rather belatedly to Cardinal Beaufort, a cynical and worldly politician, who died on 11 April 1447, leaving behind him this request: 'I will that ten thousand masses be celebrated for the repose of my soul as soon as possible after my decease.' Ten years later, the Duchess of Exeter expressed a similar pious wish: 'I will that my executors find an honest priest' (an illuminating stipulation) 'to say mass and pray for my soul, my lords soul, and all Christian souls, in the Chapel where my Body be buried, for the space of seven years next after my decease.' By the following century, however, more mundane considerations were troubling the Duchess of Northumberland, who concluded her will coyly: 'In nowise let me be opened after I am dead; I have not used to be very bold before women, much more would I be loth to come into the hands of any living man, be he physician or surgeon.'

In 1418, Ludovico Cortusio, an eminent lawyer of Padua, disinherited anyone who should weep at his funeral. (See page 41.)

After the Reformation, the clergy generally ceased to benefit on any large scale from wills. Patronage gave place to distrust, as an anti-clerical observer recorded in

1561: 'I shulde speake nothing, in the mean season, of the costly feastes and bankettes that are commonly made unto the priestes (whiche come to suche doinges from all partes, as Ravens do to a deade Carkase), in their buryinges, moneths mindes and yeares myndes.'

But if the Church was no longer favoured, prodigal gestures were still made to secular beneficiaries. Robert Dudley, Earl of Leicester, Queen Elizabeth's favourite, making his will in 1587, confessed that he had 'lived alwayes above eny livinge I hadd', and was consequently 'I knowe not howe many thousands above XXtie in debt'. Nevertheless, a courtier to the last, he contrived to bequeath to the Queen 'the jewell with three great emrodes with a faire large table diamond in the middest . . . and a rope of faire white pearles to the number of 600'. Penury seems to have been a common complaint among Elizabeth's servants. Three years later, Sir Francis Walsingham (the 'M' of the sixteenth-century Secret Service), asked in his will to 'be buryed without any suche extraordynarie ceremonyes as usuallye apperteyne to a man servinge in my place, in respect of the greatnes of my debtes, and the meane state I shall leave my wife and heire in'.

Shakespeare's will, drawn up on 25 March 1616, opened with a splendid clause, worthy of the pen of England's greatest man of letters: 'First, I commend my soul into the hands of God my creator, hoping, and assuredly believing, through the only merits of Jesus Christ my Saviour, to be made partaker of life everlasting; and my body to the earth whereof it is made.' Unfortunately, he was unable to sustain this elevated tone throughout the succeeding catalogue of domestic details. By the time he reached the tenth clause, the Bard was reduced to the bald statement: 'Item, I give unto my wife my second best bed, with the furniture.' Great artists, in fact, frequently made very practical wills. Gainsborough gave an interesting insight into his view of his vocation when he bequeathed to his nephew and disciple, Gainsborough Dupont, 'my utensils in the painting business'.

If there was one section of society, however, whose members might have been expected to lead the field in testamentary efficiency, it was surely the legal profession. Alas, nothing could be further from reality. Some of the most appallingly incompetent wills have been made by lawyers: as soon as they attempt to act on their own behalf instead of that of their clients, it might almost be said, they fall victim to a kind of jinx. It amounts to a hallowed tradition. As early as 1482, Mark Cottle, Registrar of the Prerogative Court of Canterbury (and thus the foremost custodian of wills in England) was found to have omitted the date on his own last will and testament, so that an affidavit had to be filed before it could be proved.

The Cottle Syndrome, as we may call it, turned out not to be an isolated case, but the start of an epidemic. During the eighteenth and nineteenth centuries, it affected some of the most distinguished men ever to don wig and gown. Bradley, the eighteenth-century 'patriarch of conveyancing', had his eccentric will, in which he sought to devote £40,000 to the purchase of religious tracts and other improving literature, quashed by Lord Thurlow. The will of Sir Samuel Romilly, who held the office of Solicitor-General himself and was father of another holder of the post, was found, after his death in 1818, to be execrably drafted.

When Chief Justice Saunders, another nineteenth-century legal lion, made his will, he indulged in a speculative devise, so that his three executors, Maynard, Holt, and Pollexfen — all great lawyers of their day — could not agree whether it was valid or not. Two of these same executors, Mr Serjeant Maynard and Chief Justice Holt, themselves made wills which were later subject to proceedings in Chancery.

This chronicle of legal bungling might have been thought to have reached a peak when Lord Westbury, who had been Lord High Chancellor from 1861 to 1865, died on 20 July 1873, leaving behind him a will which provoked fierce dispute.

Less than two years later, however, one of his predecessors in that highest of judicial offices, Lord St Leonards, followed him to the grave, with even worse testamentary chaos as a consequence. The irony of it was that Lord St Leonards had spent the last four years of his life revising his will. He had been at odds with his grandson and heir over his proposed marriage, and as his exasperation increased, a succession of codicils had progressively altered his will in favour of his younger son. Throughout this acrimonious process, the document itself and its growing brood of codicils was jealously guarded by the old peer, or, when he was too ill, by his daughter. It was preserved in a box to which there were just two keys; Lord St Leonards kept one on his person, the other was locked in an escritoire to which there was apparently no access.

His Lordship died at the age of ninety-four, leaving landed property amounting to more than 4,500 acres, producing an annual rental of £5,728, besides personal assets of £60,000. After his funeral, however, when the fateful box was opened, the will was not inside. It was subsequently discovered that there were no fewer than four keys in the house capable of opening the escritoire where the duplicate key of the box was kept. In these circumstances, when the case was heard in the Probate Court, the judge ruled the will lost through insecure custody, and accepted a reconstruction of it from memory by Lord St Leonards's daughter, the Hon. Charlotte Sugden, who was one of the executors and who had lived with the document long enough to be only too familiar with its contents.

With perhaps a soupçon of malice, the judge quoted from a passage in the *Handy-Book of Property Law*, written by Lord St Leonards, in which he had discouraged his readers from lodging their wills at the Probate Registry: 'If you are likely from time to time to alter your Will, I should advise you not to place it in this depository.' With the salutary example of the author's own mishap before the court, the judge commented, 'I think it is to be regretted that advice was given.'

By the turn of the century, the list of other lawyers whose wills had given rise to court proceedings read like a *Who's Who* of the bench and bar: Chief Baron Thomson, Chief Justice Eyre, Baron Cleasby, Baron Wood, Mr Serjeant Hill, Mr Justice Vaughan, the famous Chancery Counsel Vernon, Richard Preston and Thomas Braithwaite, both eminent conveyancers. Finally, at the very end of the Victorian era, yet another lawyer's will provoked litigation; the testator was Sir Francis Jeune. And what legal office had the late Sir Francis held? Quite a responsible one — he was President of the Probate, Divorce and Admiralty Division of the High Court!

One of the most alarming characteristics of wills is the ease with which they vanish, and their even more disconcerting tendency to reappear in highly dramatic circumstances. They have been discovered in every conceivable hiding-place, from weather-cocks to picture-frames. Among the curiosities which have found their way at different times to Somerset House have been a cabinet with a secret drawer, specially built by an elderly physician in the early eighteenth century to conceal his will from rapacious relatives, and a scale model of a four-poster bedstead. This model was constructed, since the original was too large to carry into court, to illustrate the exact position in which the will of a rich peer had been found tied to a bar of the bedstead leg, after his death.

Other lost wills have been recovered in the most bizarre fashion. A woman who died in Cheshire, in 1819, confessed on her death-bed that her husband, who had predeceased her four years previously, had made a will which she had concealed. After his death, she had discovered that his will benefited their daughter, to the exclusion of herself and their son, who was her favourite. She had therefore disposed of the will by placing it with her husband's body in his coffin. As a result of this ghoulish revelation, an exhumation order had to be sought to reclaim the will from the grave.

Four years may seem a long time for a will to be buried, but there is record of one which lay submerged for two and a half centuries. Its discovery took place in Massachusetts, in the United States. On 2 February 1898, a fisherman at New Bedford decided to defy the inauspicious name of the water, and cast his hook and line through the ice of Bad Luck Pond. Very shortly, thinking he had hooked a fish, he drew in his line, only to discover that his catch consisted of a rawhide case, about ten inches long and two inches in circumference. Surprise changed to amazement when he cut it open and found a well-preserved document inside. Dated 3 March 1646, it was the will of John Coffin, witnessed by Moses Trafton and Elizabeth Marsh, bequeathing two houses and two lots, near Sunderland, County Durham, England, to the testator's daughter, Mary.

A recurring, morbid preoccupation among testators was the fear of being buried alive. (See page 62.)

The question which remained to be answered was how the will of a seventeenth-century Englishman, from Sunderland, came to be lying, perfectly preserved, under the icy waters of Bad Luck Pond, in America, 252 years later? The most plausible explanation would seem to be that John Coffin was an early colonist who was attacked by hostile Indians and tried to escape across Bad Luck Pond by canoe. In his case, the Pond lived up to its name: his enemies caught up with him, killed him, and threw his body into the water. Long after Mr Coffin's much-abused person had decayed, the stout rawhide case kept the will intact, until it was recovered from the depths by an angler's chance cast. This indestructible document was deservedly sent to the Smithsonian Institute, in Washington, as an eloquent witness to the past.

Nowhere is there stronger evidence to be found of the maxim that truth is stranger than fiction than in the world of eccentric will-makers. The most far-fetched and absurd wills are the almost daily product of extravagant minds, untamed by the prospect of approaching death.

In the succeeding pages, therefore, we shall concern ourselves with a small selection of wills made by testators who committed their fancies to paper, conscripted their friends as witnesses, appended their signatures in due form, and then awaited their dissolution with the serene consciousness of duty accomplished — all, of course, after formally declaring themselves of sound mind!

Unusual Types of Will

Most people are rather afraid of wills, not just because of their association with death, but because of their legal complexity. They have a well-founded fear that a misplaced comma may lead to a total misinterpretation of their intentions. Some try to beat the lawyers at their own game by making their wills as long-winded and complicated as possible, in the vain hope that a torrent of legal-sounding phrases will exorcise the dreaded profession. This, of course, is completely self-defeating: nothing provides more meat for litigation than a do-it-yourself layman. Try as he may to bluff his way bravely, strewing 'hereuntos' and 'wheretofores' as protective mantras around him, his labour will be in vain. Like a single drop of blood in the ocean, his uselessly spilled ink will attract sharks from a wide radius.

This dread of lawyers is by no means a modern phenomenon. As long ago as 1603, Alderman Gee of Kingston-upon-Hull prefaced his exceptionally generous bequests to charity with the observation: 'So I doe now pray and humbly beseeche the gret and myghtie God to confounde and destroye al those menn lawyers and others whoever to the devil to dwel yn the pit of hel who doe or shal doe or tak upon them to alter ys my wille.' Even more defiant was Thomas Southam, a yeoman from Charlecote in Warwickshire, who made his will on 12 December 1684. 'This is my last will and testament (and I revoke all wills formerly made by me whatsoever),' he concluded firmly, 'and whether it be law or not this shall stand and noe law whatsoever shall alter it.' Despite this gauntlet thrown down to the legal establishment, the will was proved six weeks later.

Sometimes the desire to use as many formal styles as possible reduced testators to an inability to see the wood for the trees. Only a confusion of mind brought on by the mesmeric influence of legal phraseology can explain the wording of the will of John Houldin, a Derbyshire man, who wrote on 21 November 1724, 'All the rest Residue and remainder of my personal Estate I give to my dear and well beloved *wife* Sarah Houldin, *spinster.'*

There was a more businesslike tone to the will of Lieutenant-General Henry Hawley, a martinet who had been commander-in-chief in Scotland during part of the 1745 Rebellion and distinguished by his cruelty to the defeated Jacobites. 'I direct and order,' he wrote, in 1749, 'that my carcass be put anywhere . . . The priest, I conclude, will have his due; let the puppy have it. Pay the carpenter for the box. I give to my sister £5,000.' Having thus graciously discharged his obligations to the Church, cottage industry, and his own family, General Hawley went on to adopt as his son Captain William Toovey of the Royal Dragoons, whose mother had been his companion, nurse, and faithful steward. It was not to be hoped that so outspoken a testator would spare the legal fraternity and, predictably, he loosed a Parthian shot in the last clause: 'I have written this with my own hand, because I hate priests of all professions, and have the worst opinion of all members of the law.'

As civilization progressed, however, other military testators felt it incumbent upon them to bid farewell to society with some elaboration. Among such was Major-General Claude Martin, of the Bengal Civil Service, who died in 1800 after a remarkable career. Born the son of a cooper, he amassed a huge fortune and died a millionaire. The preamble to his will consisted of a long religious sermon, but his beliefs were so idiosyncratic that they could not be ascribed to any recognized Christian denomination, though they resembled a bastardized form of Catholicism. His will was such a curiosity that it was printed in a limited edition for collectors at Lyons in 1803. It comprised a quarto volume of 155 pages, 83 of which contained the main text of the will in 34 clauses, the remaining 72 pages consisting of schedules which listed the General's property and finances in detail.

It comprised a quarto volume of 155 pages.

In complete contrast, one of the shortest wills ever was proved at Lewes Probate Court in Sussex, in November 1878. It read simply: 'Mrs — to have all when I die.'

But this testament was positively verbose, compared to the briefest will on record in the English language. Frederick Charles William Thorn, commonly known as Charley Thorn, of Streatham, was taken ill suddenly and made his will on 16 May 1905. He was incapable of speech, but managed to make signs that he wanted a piece of paper. An envelope was brought, on which he scrawled 'All for mother,' then added his initials 'C.T.' His sons witnessed it just before he died and, on 22 February 1906, in the Probate Court, Sir Gorell Barnes upheld it as a valid will conveying the £8,000 estate to the widow. It is a measure of the will's brevity that if the testator had signed with his full name, instead of his

27

initials, he would have more than doubled its length. The wording was similar to that of the shortest will in the world, written in Czech — *'Vše ženĕ'* ('All to wife') — by a Herr Tausch, of Langen in Germany, in January 1967.

Unfortunately, such succinct will-makers are in a minority. The long-winded majority continue to expend ink and paper in ever more prolix documentation of their last wishes. For this school of thought, the current exemplar is Mrs Frederic Evelyn Stilwell Cook, who died on 9 January 1925. Her will, the testamentary equivalent of a Tolstoyan epic, amounted to 1,066 probate folios of 90 words each, bound in four gilt-edged volumes — total length 95,940 words.

This is the longest will recorded so far, but testators are a competitive breed and it seems safe to assume that an ambitious rival will soon seek to upset Mrs Cook's record and break the testamentary sound barrier of 100,000 words.

The popular notion of a will conjures up visions of parchment, Gothic script, wax seals, stamps, and signatures embellished with Italic flourishes. It is an impressive image, but hardly romantic and certainly not poetic. Yet the surprising truth is that quite a number of people have chosen to write their wills in verse. Even more remarkably, these rhyming wills have mostly been the testators' first attempts at poetry and have been upheld as valid and admitted to probate.

The earliest verse will in England was made in the sixteenth century by William Hunnis, who was Chapel Master to Queen Elizabeth and so an unlikely candidate for such frivolity — or, indeed, for the improvidence to which he confessed in the last line:

> To God my soule I do bequeathe, because it is his owen,
> My body to be layd in grave, where to my friends best knowen;
> Executors I will none make, thereby great stryfe may grow,

Because the goods that I shall leave wyll not pay all I
   owe.

Few people were in a hurry to imitate William Hunnis
until the eighteenth century, when the flowering of the
Augustan age appears to have inspired a spate of poetic
wills. John Hedges, a bachelor, of St George's parish,
Hanover Square, died at Finchley in 1737, when his will
was discovered to read as follows:

   This fifth day of May,
   Being airy and gay,
   To hyp not inclined,
   But of vigorous mind,
   And my body in health,
   I'll dispose of my wealth . . .

   I do therefore enjoin,
   And strictly command,
   As witness my hand,

That nought I have got,
Be brought to hotch-pot;
And I give and devise,
Much as in me lies,
To the son of my mother,
My own dear brother,
To have and to hold
All my silver and gold,
As th' affectionate pledges
Of his brother, JOHN HEDGES.

Despite its unusual form, this will contained all the classic components — date, declaration of sound mind, and signature — so that administration was duly granted on 13 July 1737.

More self-consciously literary was the composition of Nathaniel Lloyd, of Twickenham, who took up his pen on 16 October 1769, and expressed himself in the following terms:

What I am going to bequeath,
When this frail spark submits to death;
But still I hope the spark divine
With its congenial stars shall shine;
My good Executors, fulfil,
I pray ye, fairly, my last will,
With first and second codicil.

There then followed various bequests, including:

To Vere, Earl Poulett's second son,
Who dearly loves a little fun . . .

One hundred pounds to my niece, Tuder
(With loving eyes one Matthew view'd her) . . .

Even Lady Poulett's maidservants, Sally Crouch and Mary Lee, received legacies:

The first, ten pounds: the other twenty;
And, girls, I hope that will content ye.

Then Mr Lloyd summarized his disposition.

In seventeen hundred, sixty-nine,
This with my hand I write and sign,
The sixteenth day of fair October,
In merry mood, but sound and sober;
Past my threescore-and-fifteenth year,
With spirits gay and conscience clear,
Joyous and frolicsome, though old,
And like this day — serene, but cold;
To foes well-wishing, and to friends most kind,
In perfect charity with all mankind.

But this amateur poet was evidently aware of his literary shortcomings, for he then bolstered up his own verse by annexing ten lines of Matthew Prior (frankly acknowledged) to provide an impressive climax to his testament.

In the following year, a rhyming will of rather different character was made by William Hickington, from Pocklington (a conjunction of names which rendered his poetic vocation almost inevitable). For Mr Hickington differed from most versifying testators in being a regular practitioner of poetry and his collected works were published fifty years later. His will, therefore, was appropriately Bohemian in mood and aggressively flouted bourgeois morality:

This is my last will,
I insist on it still,
So sneer on and welcome,
And e'en laugh your fill.
I, William Hickington,
Poet, of Pocklington,
Do give and bequeath
As free as I breathe
To thee, Mary Jarum,
The queen of my harem,
My cash and my cattle,
With every chattel,
To have and to hold,

31

Come heat or come cold,
Sans hindrance or strife,
Though thou art not my wife;
As witness my hand,
Just here as I stand,
The twelve day of July,
In the year seventy.
Signed,
WILLIAM HICKINGTON

As the text betrays, the poet was anxious to offset the flippant medium of verse with some seasoning of legal language; in the event, he seems to have settled for a happy compromise between the phraseology of the marriage service (audacious in the circumstances) and the formula on a passport. Despite its advertisement of Mr Hickington's scandalous domestic arrangements, the will was proved in the Deanery Court at York.

Long before the twentieth century, office workers entertained escapist fantasies to lighten their days. Two hundred years ago, the equivalent dream to winning the football pools was that of becoming a poet. Will Jackett, of Islington, was employed as a principal clerk by Messrs Fuller and Co. When he suddenly dropped dead one day at the Royal Exchange, it was discovered that he had indulged a secret romanticism by composing a poetic will.

I give and bequeath
(When I'm laid underneath)
To my two loving sisters most dear
The whole of my store,
Were it twice as much more,
Which God's goodness has granted me here.

And that none may prevent
This my will and intent,
Or occasion the least of law racket,
With a solemn appeal,
I confirm, sign, and seal
This the true act and deed of Will Jackett.

Although his verse was light-hearted and informal, Mr Jackett was scrupulous in observing legal niceties: two footnotes identified his sisters by name as Elizabeth and Ann, and inserted the solemn preamble: 'In the name of God, Amen.' This diligence was rewarded when the will was proved at Doctors' Commons on 17 July 1789.

It was mostly men who chose to write their wills in rhyme, but the fair sex could turn out a competent iambic tetrameter when they felt the urge, as is proved by the will of Monica Swiney:

> Of this I never will repent,
> 'Tis my last Will and testament,
> If much or little — nay, my all —
> I give my brother, Matthew Gall;
> And this will hinder any pother
> By sister Stritch or Mic, our brother:
> Yet stop! should Mat die before Mic,
> And that may happen, for Death's quick,
> I then bequeath my worldly store
> To brother Mic for evermore;
> But should I outlive my brothers,
> It's fit that then I think of others.
> Matthew has sons, and daughters too,
> 'Tis all their own, were it Peru.
> Pray, Mr Forrest, don't sit still,
> But witness this as my last Will.

This too was successfully proved at Doctors' Commons.

A rhyming will was obviously a device which would appeal to the Irish temperament and, sure enough, a schoolmaster called Pat O'Kelly made a contribution to testamentary verse, written appropriately in an exercise-book:

> I, having neither kith nor kin,
> Bequeath all I have named herein
> To Harriet my dearest wife,
> To have and hold as hers for life.
> While in good health, and sound in mind,
> This codicil I've undersigned.

The majority of poetic testators kept their wills short, probably because they soon ran out of inspiration or suitable rhymes. A Suffolk gentleman, however, named William Ruffell, produced a more ambitious composition of epic length. In the early couplets he indulged in that abuse of the legal profession which was common to wills in prose or verse.

To employ an attorney I ne'er was inclin'd,
They are pests to society, sharks of mankind.
To avoid that base tribe my own will I now draw,
May I ever escape coming under their paw.

Then, after bequeathing his landed property to his nephew, Mr Ruffell left a more dubious legacy to his sister.

To my loving, kind sister I give and bequeath,
For her tender regard, when this world I shall leave,
If she choose to accept it, my rump-bone may take,
And tip it with silver, a whistle to make.

He was less indulgent, however, towards his brother-in-law.

My brother-in-law is a strange-tempered dog;
He's as fierce as a tiger, in manners a hog;
A petty tyrant at home, his frowns how they dread;
Two ideas at once never entered his head.

So, after some more reflections in this vein, his brother-in-law was cut off with a shilling. Mr Ruffell was so proud of this literary effort, drawn up on 18 March 1803, that he distributed copies of it among his friends.

Less than two years later, on 13 December 1804, Joshua West, of the Six Clerks' Office in Chancery Lane (not normally a power-house of poesy), drew up his will in a form that must have surprised his colleagues.

Perhaps I died not worth a groat;
But should I die worth something more,
Then I give that, and my best coat,

And all my manuscripts in store,
To those who shall the goodness have
   To cause my poor remains to rest
Within a decent shell and grave.
   This is the will of Joshua West.

The manuscripts legally conveyed by this will were actually quite valuable. But if such frivolity was unexpected in a clerk, it was even more startling to find a member of the hated legal fraternity, a London attorney called Smithers, defying all the canons of his caste and making a brief, clear, good-natured will in verse:

As to all the worldly goods I have in store,
I leave to my beloved wife and hers for evermore;
I give all freely, I no limit fix,
This is my will, and she executrix.

In contrast to such simplicity, the most elaborate rhyming will of all time was composed by an undergraduate of Trinity College, Dublin, in the early nineteenth century. Having drunk himself almost to death on brandy, he redeemed his academic record in his last hours by writing a macaronic will, no less, with alternate lines in Latin and English, addressed to his best friend. It began:

Cum ita semper me amares,
[Since by you I've long been cherished,]
How to regard you all my care is;

Consilium tibi do imprimis,
[First of all I must admonish,]
For I believe but short my time is;

Amice admodum amande,
[My friend, deserving of me kindly,]
Pray thee leave off thy drinking brandy . . .

Then, after bequeathing his clothes, footwear, books, and even his muse to his friend, the testator concluded in more romantic vein:

Spero quod his contentus eris,
[I hope that this provision pleases,]
For I've a friend almost as dear is;

Vale, ne plus tibi detur,
[Farewell, before your share grows greater,]
But send her up, Jack, if you meet her.

By the middle of the nineteenth century, however, Mr Smithers, the uxorious attorney, was finding imitators within the legal profession. John Cooper Grocott, an octogenarian solicitor from Liverpool, who was also author of a best-selling book entitled *An Index of Familiar Quotation, Ancient and Modern*, made his will on 26 January 1835. With his professional expertise he was able to gild his verses with impressive technical jargon.

I therefore give to my dear Wife
All my Estates, to keep for life,
Real and Personal, Profits, Rents,
Messuages, Lands, and Tenements;
After her death, I give the whole
Unto my Children, one and all,
To take as 'Tenants in Common' do,
Not as 'Joint Tenants', 'per mie — per tout'.

Later, in less formal tones, he exclaimed:

And now, my Wife, my hopes I fix
On thee, my Sole Executrix —
My truest, best, and to the end
My faithful Partner, 'Crown', and Friend.

To maintain the poetic quality to the very end, there was even a separate stanza beneath which the witnesses placed their signatures:

This Will was published, sealed and sign'd,
By the Testator, in his right mind,
In presence of us, who, at his request,
Have written our names these facts to attest.

So far, it was the educated classes who had been responsible for wills written in rhyme. Yet one of the most striking poetic wills was composed by one James Bigsby, a labourer from Manningtree in Essex, who, as one of the Victorian poor, might not have been expected to have a sufficiently frivolous temperament (especially on his death-bed) to dictate such a trifle. Dated 4 February 1839, the preamble ran:

As I feel very queer my will I now make;
Write it down, Joseph Finch, and make no mistake.

After reviewing the members of his family who had a claim on him, he left various household effects to his wife; the earlier items were commonplace, but then the inventory began to assume rather a military character:

I also bequeath to Lydia my wife
A box in the cupboard, a sword, gun, and knife,
And the harmless old pistol without any lock,
Which no man can fire off, for 'tis minus a cock.

Then, after many other small legacies:

And to Uncle Sam Bigsby I bequeath my high boots,
The pickaxe and mattock with which I stubbed roots.
And poor Uncle Gregory, with the whole of my heart,
I give for a bedstead the back of the cart.

It is gratifying to be able to record that the back of the cart enjoyed many years' service as a bedstead in the Bigsbys' cottage.

There was no eclipse of the poetic muse during the eventful years of Victoria's reign. On 10 August 1891, John Powell made a further contribution to the versifying tradition.

When my Wife's a Widow of me bereft,
She shall inherit all I've left;
And when she's finished her career,
It shall then go to my Daughters dear.

In equal shares to save all bother,
Not flesh to one and fish the other.
They all are kind and dear to me,
So no distinction shall there be.

In the twentieth century, too, inspiration has not failed the cultivated testator, even amid the most up-to-date technological innovations. Thus, an American woman who recently recorded her will on video-tape, after leaving all she possessed to her husband, concluded with these elevating lines:

Don't go to Vegas or play with stock,
Or drink much after six o'clock,
Or party far into the night;
You'll join me if you don't live right.
And, please, when all my songs are sung —
Don't fall for someone cute and young!

After the many sublime lyrics already quoted, it is painful to descend to the ridiculous. But it has to be placed on record, in the interests of scholarship, that one testator, whose muse did not run to a poetic will, had the poor taste to make a punning one. The culprit was a gentleman from Kent who, after disposing of an estate worth £10,091 and ten pence, gave the following excruciating burial instructions: 'The coffin is to be of red fir. I *pine* for nothing better. Even this may be thought a *deal* too good, though certainly not very *spruce* . . .' Among fanciful testators, this was surely a candidate for the wooden spoon.

Whatever form the remainder of a will may take, the one indispensable part of the wording is the signature. Sometimes it is amplified by a seal; the very 'compleat' will of Izaac Walton, the pioneering angler, dated 24 October 1683, was sealed with a curious device depicting Christ crucified on an anchor.

In the case of one testator, the signature itself was a

curiosity — 'Time of Day', the name of a man whose will was recorded in due form at Somerset House. His surname was Day and his parents, who apparently had a puckish sense of humour, had launched him on his slide down the razor-blade of life by christening him 'Time Of'. With parents like that, he could hardly be expected to lavish legacies sympathetically on orphans.

The simple rule is: no signature, no will. A Swiss-born officer of the Royal Artillery, named Chalon, died intestate in 1860, although he had drawn up a detailed will. The problem was that he had neither signed it nor had it witnessed, because of a superstitious fear that he would die as soon as it was completed. This superstition was widespread; Francis Bacon refers to it in his writings, as does Hazlitt, and Boswell reveals that Dr Johnson was reluctant to make his will for the same reason.

On the other hand, a valid signature need not be written — a thumbprint has been recognized as adequate. An illiterate testator called James Finn, from Liverpool, died on 25 July 1935, after dictating his will to a clergyman who then smeared the dying man's thumb with ink and pressed it on to the paper. When probate was sought, it was explained that the clergyman had worked overseas, where it was common practice for natives to sign their wills in this way; learned counsel also quoted a precedent from 1839. Mr Justice Langton granted probate, but added with evident disgruntlement, 'The method adopted in the present case, however, does not commend itself to me at all.' It is also essential for the signature to be on the will itself. George Bean, of Doncaster, who made his will on 23 May 1940, on a printed form, correctly witnessed, wrote his name and address on the envelope containing the document, but not in the space provided on the will-form. After his death three years later, it was ruled invalid.

But if the law is inflexible in the matter of signatures, it is surprisingly elastic as regards the physical format of a last will and testament. No real-life will-maker has gone quite so far as the fictitious case in Rider Haggard's novel

39

Mr Meeson's Will, where the testament in question was tattooed on a girl's back; but the story of the man who chalked his will on a stable-door, which then had to be unhinged (as, one suspects, the testator may also have been) and carried into court for probate, has long since entered legal mythology.

. . . Chalked his will on a stable-door.

Sometimes an emergency dictated unusual forms of will. In 1801, an apothecary serving with the British forces in Aboukir Bay fell ill and made his will, in the form of a letter to his colleague, the surgeon on board the flagship. Dated Aboukir, 1 July 1801, it began conversationally, 'Being now aflickted with the Plague, the Scourge of Mankind, which will probably soon terminate my existence . . .' This preamble terrified the surgeon: the letter was almost certainly a source of infection and his one desire was to rid himself of it. He retained sufficient judgement, however, to realize that to destroy a will would be criminal. So he made a copy and placed the original in a bottle of spirit which he sealed and brought home to England. In the meantime, the unhappy apothecary had died, so his will was brought to probate.

But when the bottle was opened, the surgeon-executor was embarrassed to discover that the strong spirit had dissolved the writing on the will. In these circumstances, and respecting the surgeon's professional concern for public health, the court accepted the copy as valid.

Even more dramatic was the codicil to Nelson's will, written in a diary on the morning of Trafalgar and dated: 'October the twenty-first, one thousand eight hundred and five, then in sight of the Combined Fleets of France and Spain distant about ten miles.' Solemnly witnessed by Captains Hardy and Blackwood, the codicil was odd not only in being scribbled in a pocket-book, but also in the bequest it conveyed. After rehearsing the lady's long record of patriotic service, Nelson concluded: 'I leave Emma Lady Hamilton, therefore, a Legacy to my King and Country . . .' It was a gesture which accorded with Lady Hamilton's own well-known generosity in dispensing consolation to her countrymen; unfortunately, it is not recorded whether George III ever took possession of his unexpected windfall.

Compression of the text of their wills seems to have been the main aim of some testators. Early this century, for example, probate was granted to a will engraved by a naval stoker on his metal identity-disc. But the supreme example was a will written on an eggshell. The testator in this case was a maritime pilot called James Barnes, who died on 18 June 1925, leaving an estate worth £5,500. He had made a conventional will in 1920, but when his widow cleaned out his bedroom, she found on top of the wardrobe the hollow shell of a hen's egg which had been blown, and written on it in indelible ink: '17 — — 1925. Mag. Everything i possess — — — J.B.'

Since 'Mag' was her name and this will was more favourable to her than the one made in 1920, Mrs Barnes claimed that the inscription on the egg was the privileged will of a mariner, not requiring witnesses, and superseding any earlier testament. But Lord Merrivale, in giving judgement, pointed out that, as Mr Barnes had been a pilot on the Manchester Ship Canal and lived on

. . . Will written on an egg.

shore in a bungalow, he could hardly be numbered among those in peril on the sea, as envisaged by the Wills Act of 1837. Moreover, since the widow's name was not preceded by the preposition 'to', implying a donation, the wording did not constitute a will. So the eggshell was ruled invalid. It must be stressed, however, that the use of the eggshell was not what invalidated the will, so that intending egg-testators should not be discouraged by this precedent.

In a crisis, testators will grasp at anything. George W. Hazeltine, a rich American who died at the age of eighty-six, spent his last days in a Los Angeles hospital, where he became very attached to two of his nurses, Lillian Pelkey and Madeline Higgins. So he announced his intention of making a new will, in order to leave $10,000 to each of them. The two nurses protested against this proposal, but agreed to humour the old man. Since there was no writing-paper available (for a Californian hospital, the establishment seems to have been strangely ill-provided!), Nurse Pelkey wrote the will on her underwear, which Mr Hazeltine then gratefully signed, the Misses Pelkey and Higgins acting as witnesses. Ironically, under Californian law, this debarred both of them from receiving their legacies, but neither of them wished to do so in any case. This unusual will, however, was admitted to probate, and another beneficiary, a great-niece of the testator who was under no disqualification, inherited the estate by its terms. Lingerie also featured prominently in the will of Ellen Collins, of Philadelphia, in 1932: 'I give, devise, and bequeath my white flannel embroidered petticoat, made by Mrs Lowry, to Mr Albert Cummings absolutely.' Tragically, Mr Cummings died before his intending benefactress (who presumably had some reason to believe that he coveted her petticoat), so that he never had the opportunity of entering into his inheritance.

Another man, who died in Los Angeles, apparently without making a will, left estate equivalent to £3,000. Shortly afterwards, a neighbour borrowed the deceased's step-ladder and found this moving testament scribbled on one rung: 'December 2nd, 1933. I love her. Give my all to Mrs Gotts. She is my good spirit.' The ladder was duly proved.

. . . Made a gramophone record of his will.

A technological breakthrough came in 1937 when a man in Brisbane, Australia, made a gramophone record of his will, reinforcing the old legal tag that 'a will speaks from death'. Nowadays, in both Britain and America, this idea has been further developed so that some lawyers offer their clients facilities for recording their wills on video-tape, though these are not legally enforceable unless accompanied by a written text as well. In such video recordings, testators are allowed to indulge their sense of the dramatic — like one man who insisted on donning a shroud and dictating his will from a coffin.

A will written on the back of a Christmas card.

As all these examples show, provided the basic legal requirements are met, a will is valid when inscribed upon an unconventional object; as recently as 1959, the courts upheld a will written on the back of a Christmas card. There is something peculiarly indestructible about wills: the hazards which they have survived are remarkable. Rats are especially partial to a diet of testamentary papers. In 1646, the will of a Mr Etheringham was 'gnawn all to pieces with rats', but the clerk to whom it had been entrusted 'with help of the pieces, and of his memory and other witnesses, caused it to be proved in the Ecclesiastical Court'. A will made by a Belfast woman in 1911 was locked away in a drawer for thirteen years. When the drawer was opened after her death, there was nothing left of the will, except a few scraps, rats having devoured it. With Irish enterprise, however, a copy was patched up out of the shreds and the memory of witnesses, and this attested copy was eventually admitted to probate in Belfast, on 27 February 1925.

A will has even survived shipwreck. It was made by a labourer who died at Canterbury, New Zealand, in 1868, leaving his entire savings of £300 in the British Post Office to his wife, who lived at Rye in Sussex. The will was an impressive parchment, bearing the seal of the Supreme Court of New Zealand. After the due processes of law had been carried out in the Antipodes, the deceased's solicitor in Auckland despatched the will to a lawyer in London, so that Letters of Administration could be taken out in England. Unfortunately, it was carried on the mail steamer *Schiller*, which was wrecked on the Scilly Isles on 7 May 1875. Shortly afterwards, however, a Cornish fisherman mending his nets on the beach saw a packet washed ashore, which proved to be the will from New Zealand. Though reduced to a saturated pulp, the parchment was painstakingly separated and stretched so that, after all its vicissitudes, it finally joined other curious, but valid, documents at Somerset House.

It is almost commonplace for mutilated wills to be admitted to probate. In 1953, the will of Mrs Louisa Scott Skrimshire, who had died five years earlier at the age of eighty-two, was upheld in the Probate Division, although it had been torn into many pieces and then stuck together again. Mr Justice Barnard commented understandingly, 'Old ladies do such odd things.' His Lordship then indulged in an imaginative reconstruction of the accident: 'She may have torn it up accidentally and then thought, "Oh dear, oh dear", and wrapped up the pieces, believing the will to be still good.'

At least Mrs Skrimshire tried to repair the damage she had done, unlike Mrs Gertrude Aynsley, of Newcastle upon Tyne, who tore up her will while she was in a nursing home and her state of mind was confused. The will, disposing of an estate of £35,000, was ripped up into more than forty fragments. So Mr Justice Megarry, who heard the case on 5 February 1973, retired to his room at the High Court for an hour and reassembled the jigsaw-puzzle will. Every piece was there and the document was perfect when fitted together, so that the judge returned triumphantly to court and pronounced the will valid. It was a problem and a solution which would have delighted Rider Haggard and all the eclectic company of versifying testators and eggshell and lingerie signatories who had long since been admitted to probate.

Bizarre Burial Instructions

Of all the bequests which can feature in a will, the one which inspires the highest flights of fancy is the disposal of the object which has been dearest to the testator in life — Number One, the mortal remains of his own person. Well, you might think, and quite right too! Even if a chap has nothing else to leave, surely he at least has the right to dispose of his own body. You would be wrong: he hasn't. In Britain at any rate, a person has no rights over his body after the moment of death. The only way he can control his burial arrangements, therefore, is to bribe his own flesh-and-blood with a bequest made conditional on their carrying out his wishes. If they refuse to do so, then they forfeit their share of his worldly goods, but they can do what they like — provided it is legal and decent — with his body.

The most sensational burial request to hit world headlines in recent years was that of Mrs Sandra West, widow of Ike West, a Texas oil millionaire. When she died in March 1977, at the age of thirty-seven, she left her entire $2.8 million estate to her brother-in-law Sol West, on condition that he obeyed her rather original burial instructions: she was to be dressed in her lace nightgown and placed in her favourite car, a blue 1964 Ferrari, 'with the seat slanted comfortably'. To frustrate thieves, the Ferrari was then to be packed in a wood and steel container and encased in concrete, before being interred in the family plot. If her brother-in-law failed to carry out this request, he was only to inherit a meagre $10,000. The will was challenged, but a Los Angeles court ruled that the request, though unusual, was lawful. 'The average person,' the judge declared, 'has a right to dispose of his or her own remains as he or she sees fit, if it does not violate the law.' So Mrs West was duly buried in her

Buried in her blue Ferrari.

Ferrari in the family grave at San Antonio, Texas, on 19 May 1977, in a ceremony described by the undertaker as 'discreet and dignified'. The dead woman's nurse explained that she had got the idea for her burial from reading about the tombs of the Pharaohs 'with their possessions, their servants and whatever'.

For the last thousand years, wills have betrayed an obsessive anxiety among testators about their burial arrangements. Funeral instructions have ranged from a modesty bordering on masochism, to downright megalomania. Humble wills included that of Duke Richard the Fearless of Normandy, in 996, who said: 'I wish to be buried in front of the church-door, so that I may be trodden under foot by all those entering the church.' In 1282, another French nobleman, Guillaume de Champlitte, Vicomte de Dijon, made an identical

48

request, as his father had done before him. Other members of the French aristocracy, however, valued themselves more highly. The Comte du Châtelet, who died about the same time, ordered that a pillar in the church at Neufchâteau should be hollowed out and his body buried upright inside it, 'in order that the vulgar may not walk upon me'.

Some people were preoccupied with the actual funeral service. Cheerful souls hated the thought of their friends being plunged into gloom by their obsequies. So, in 1418, Ludovico Cortusio, an eminent lawyer of Padua, did something about it. In his will he disinherited·anyone who should weep at his funeral, appointing whoever laughed most heartily as his principal heir. The church was to be festooned with flowers, all the musicians of the town were to play and his bier, draped in brightly-coloured cloth, was to be carried by twelve young girls dressed in green and singing lively songs. The light-hearted citizens of Padua saw to it that Signor Cortusio had his way. In similar vein, in Burgundy, in 1456, the Seigneur de Beaumont forbade sober colours at his funeral and directed that fifteen girls in white gowns with red hoods should walk in front of his body. The will of Philippe Bouton, bailiff of Dijon, in 1515, requested that fourteen girls clothed in green should attend his funeral — our ancestors seem to have had a positive fetish about girls in green! (In fact green was popular at funerals, as it was the colour of hope.)

Sometimes there was an element of propaganda about funeral instructions. Benjamin Dod, a linen-draper killed by a fall from his horse, gave vent to his High Church prejudices in his will: 'I will have no Presbyterians, moderate Low-churchmen, or occasional Conformists, to be at, or have anything to do with, my funeral. I die in the faith of the true Catholick Church.' Nor was religion the only kind of fanaticism displayed in burial directions. Margaret Thompson, a snuff addict, drew up her will in 1777, in which she ordered her coffin to be filled up with Scotch snuff until it completely covered her body. Her bearers were to be six notable snuff-takers from the parish of St James's, Westminster, the clergyman was to walk in front of the coffin, taking snuff as he progressed, and her servant was to scatter generous quantities of the drug on the ground and among the onlookers; altogether, a sure-fire recipe for a breach of the peace.

Sometimes there was an element of propaganda.

A century later, a Dutchman named Klaës, popularly known as the King of Smokers, died near Rotterdam. In his will, he invited all the smokers in Holland to his funeral, each to be presented with 10 lbs of tobacco and two Dutch pipes, engraved with the testator's name, arms, and date of death. The mourners were to keep their pipes lit throughout the funeral ceremony, and then empty the ashes on the coffin, which, though made of oak, was to be lined with the cedar of his old Havannah cigar boxes. A packet of Dutch tobacco and a box of French caporal were to be placed at the foot of the coffin, while his favourite pipe, a box of matches, a flint and steel, and some tinder were to be laid at his side, since, as Mynheer Klaës portentously declared, there was no knowing what might happen. He left bequests of tobacco and beer to the poor of the neighbourhood, an appropriate gesture, since it was estimated that during his eighty years' lifetime Mr Klaës had smoked more than four tons of tobacco and drunk about 500,000 quarts of beer.

In contrast, one Clegg, a conjuror from Rochdale (not generally thought of as a magical environment), specifically excluded snuff-takers and smokers from his funeral, likewise all women. The proceedings, in fact, bore more resemblance to a pre-nuptial stag party than a conventional funeral. Sixty guests, regaled by fiddlers, were to dance (the absence of women being no deterrent to the men of Rochdale) and make merry. Spiced buns, ale and gin were to be laid on and the stirring tune 'Britons, strike home!' was to be played on the way to the graveyard. The curate was to bring up the rear of the funeral procession, riding on an ass, a fee of one guinea being offered as an inducement to his cooperation. No one was to weep and, after the interment, the entire company was asked to repair to the deceased's favourite public house, there to eat and drink to the amount of thirty shillings, at the expense of Mr Clegg's estate. A kindred spirit was a London dyer who lived in Golden Square. To ward off melancholy, the mourners at his funeral were directed to stop at the Blue Boar public house, Westminster, and drink a gallon of ale outside the door, repeating the process at the Jolly Sawyers in Lambeth Walk; finally, they were also to carry a bottle of gin and drink it over his body as it was lowered into the grave.

It is in the actual instructions for interment, however, that testators have given widest rein to their imaginations. Viewed in historical perspective, Mrs Sandra West, embedded in concrete in her blue Ferrari, seems relatively humdrum.

It was during the eighteenth century that burial instructions, in harmony with the age, became appropriately baroque. On 1 February 1721, a Hertfordshire farmer died, leaving a will which startled his family. In it he revealed that his 'death' was in reality only a long sleep which would last for thirty years, after which he would come back to life. Accordingly, he left his estate, worth £400 a year, to his two brothers and, after them, to his

51

nephew, for a limited term of thirty years, since he proposed, reasonably enough, to resume the use of his own property after his resurrection. The bequests were conditional on the heirs agreeing to suspend his coffin from a beam in his barn, the lid not to be nailed down, but locked, with the key inside. He would thus be able simply to let himself out when he woke up, without the embarrassment of finding himself imprisoned in his now superfluous coffin. These instructions were carried out, but when the thirty years had passed the Hertfordshire Rip Van Winkle disappointed expectations by failing to waken. His nephew, who had by then inherited the property, conscientiously allowed him an extra four days' grace before depositing the coffin in an ordinary grave.

This episode, however, revolutionized the burial customs of Hertfordshire: it opened the eyes of this rural community to the vast potential of sepulchral idio-syncrasy. For it cannot have been pure coincidence that just three years later, at Stevenage in the same county, Henry Trigg similarly departed from convention in his burial directions: 'And as to my body, I commit it to the west end of my hovel, to be decently laid there upon a floor erected there by my executor for this same purpose . . .' Mr Trigg — honest fellow — had no exotic expectations of awakening after thirty years, but contented himself with established Christian doctrine concerning his body, 'nothing doubting but at the general resurrection I shall receive the same again by the mighty power of God'. Since his property was large and the conditions in the will were watertight, his brother and heir complied with his wishes.

Mad Jack Fuller, whose nickname may give a clue to his motives, lived up to the image of an eccentric eighteenth-century squire, even in death. He belonged to a family long-settled at Brightling in Sussex; another member was a medical pioneer who published the first text-book which explained authoritatively how to dis-tinguish measles-spots from flea-bites, a major problem in eighteenth-century diagnosis. When he died, Mad Jack was walled-up in a large stone tomb, his body in a seated position, with a bottle and a bird (of the feathered variety) to keep him company.

However, the Rev Langton Freeman, who lived at Whilton in Northamptonshire, went one better. His meanness was legendary and, although he had a comfortable income, he had been known to cadge his Sunday dinner from a poor labourer. He wrote his will on 16 September 1783, in which he committed the only extravagance of his frugal existence. His corpse, he directed, was to remain undisturbed on his death-bed until it began to grow offensive.

> And then I would be carried or laid in the same bed, decently and privately, in the summer-house now erected in the garden belonging to the dwelling-house, where I now inhabit in Whilton aforesaid, and to be laid in the same bed there, with all the appurtenances thereto belonging; and to be wrapped in a strong, double winding-sheet, and in all other respects to be interred as near as may be to the description we receive in Holy Scripture of our Saviour's burial.

The doors and windows of the summer-house were to be bolted and shuttered, evergreens were to be planted around it and it was to be fenced-off with palings painted dark blue. The reverend miser bequeathed the manor of Whilton to his nephew in return for honouring this request. Nearly eighty years later, when the summer-house had become dilapidated, some men climbed in through a hole in the roof and found the Rev. Langton Freeman, 'a dried up, skinny figure, having apparently the consistence of leather, with one arm laid across the chest, and the other hanging down the body', still in occupation and quite incorrupt — which was more than could be said of him in life.

In 1800, Captain Thomas Backhouse, formerly of the East India Company and a well-known Buckinghamshire eccentric, was buried near Great Missenden in a mausoleum of his own construction. It was a flat-topped pyramid built of flints and bricks, about eleven feet square at the base, rising perpendicularly for the first five feet, then tapering. Bluff old soldier that he was, Captain Backhouse had a deep distrust of graveyards. 'I'll have nothing to do with the church or the churchyard!' he declared. 'Bury me there, in my own wood on the hill, and my sword with me, and I'll defy all the evil spirits in existence to injure me!' Captain Backhouse had his wish. His sword was placed with him in the coffin, which was then stood upright within the western wall of the mausoleum and bricked-up. Seven years later, however, one of his three illegitimate sons (Captain Backhouse distrusted marriage as well as graveyards) returned from India. Although he was a lieutenant-general and so might have been expected to approve of this sepulchral sentry-duty, he had his father's body removed from the mausoleum and buried in Great Missenden churchyard, on 8 August 1807. Apparently Captain Backhouse had neglected to lay down inescapable conditions in his will.

The East India Company seems to have attracted more than its fair share of original characters; equally bizarre, but more financially remunerative, were the burial arrangements made for his wife by Major Hook, another of the Company's officers, during the last century. Mrs Hook had come into a life annuity, whose terms stated: 'And the same shall be paid to her as long as she is above ground.' When she died, therefore, the resourceful Major placed her body in a glass case and preserved it in a room devoted 'to her sole and separate use'. By this touching device, Mrs Hook remained above ground and the Major continued to enjoy both her companionship and her annuity for a further thirty years.

The ultimate in self-indulgent burial requests was made by a Monsieur Helloin, a magistrate and landowner from near Caen, in Normandy, in 1828. He was famous as the laziest and most imperturbable man in France. A bachelor (which possibly explains his habitual state of unruffled serenity), he spent his entire life either in bed or lying on a sofa. He even heard lawsuits in his bedroom, giving judgement from a recumbent position. Monsieur Helloin was determined that even death should not disrupt his tranquillity, so he made a will in which he insisted on being buried at night, still in his bed with all its furnishings intact, and in whatever position his body happened to assume at the moment of death.

. . . Buried at night still in his bed.

His desires were met, but an exceptionally large hole had to be dug to accommodate the bedstead, and boards were laid over it to prevent soil falling on to Monsieur Helloin when the grave was filled in, lest his repose might be disturbed for the first time ever.

You might feel, of course, that some of these unusual burial requests may have had a serious philosophical motivation behind them and that it is blinkered and intolerant to dismiss them as the whims of cranks. Consider, then, the will of a famous philosopher. Jeremy Bentham bequeathed his body to his friend Dr Southwood Smith, with instructions that it was to be preserved in a box, fully-clothed and even equipped with his hazel walking-stick, named Dapple after a favourite horse. 'If it should so happen that my personal friends and other Disciples should be disposed to meet together,' the great man observed modestly, 'for the purpose of commemorating the Founder of the greatest happiness system of morals and legislation my executor will from time to time cause to be conveyed to the room in which they meet the said Box or case with the contents there to be stationed in such part of the room as to the assembled company shall seem meet.'

Southwood Smith made an honest effort to carry out Bentham's wishes when he died in 1832. 'I endeavoured to preserve the head untouched,' he recorded, 'merely drawing away the fluids by placing it under an air-pump over sulphuric acid. By this means the head was rendered as hard as the skulls of the New Zealanders' (an anthropological observation, one hopes, rather than an expression of prejudice against colonials), 'but all expression was gone, of course.' So he commissioned a French artist to model the head in wax, fitted it on to the skeleton and had the whole dignified ensemble stuffed and dressed in Bentham's clothes. Then, seated in an armchair and grasping the trusty Dapple, the mummified philosopher found a home in a mahogany case with glass doors, in Smith's house in Finsbury Square. Later he was transferred to the dining-room of University College, London, where he appears to have merged harmoniously with the other dons; he remains in the college to this day. It is probably superfluous to note that Bentham was, of course, the founder of the Utilitarian philosophy, which assessed all social behaviour by its usefulness.

Not every such testator chose to bequeath his entire body: some were more selective. Two such cases occurred in America in the last century, both as expressions of an intense loyalty. John Reed worked for forty-four years as gas-lighter at the Walnut Street Theatre in Philadelphia without missing a single performance. The secret which he cherished all his life, however, and never divulged on this side of the grave, was that he was stage-struck. So, in his will, he finally found a means of realizing his ambition to tread the boards, and in a Shakespearian role, no less:

My head to be separated from my body immediately

after my death; the latter to be buried in a grave; the former, duly macerated and prepared, to be brought to the theatre, where I have served all my life, and to be employed to represent the skull of Yorick — and to this end I bequeath my head to the properties.

'. . . To represent the skull of Yorick.'

But even Mr Reed's devotion to the theatre paled into insignificance beside the fanatical patriotism which animated Mr S. Sanborn, a Massachusetts hatter (and so a member of a profession whose eccentricity is proverbial), who bequeathed his body to Harvard University in 1871. His will requested that it be used for anatomical study by the university's two eminent professors, Oliver Wendell Holmes and Louis Agassiz — an enlightened gesture, showing Mr Sanborn to be a friend of scientific progress.

In a further clause, however, he betrayed a more primitive spirit. His skin was to be made into two drumheads and given to his friend and fellow-patriot, Warren Simpson, drummer of Cohapel, on condition that he should go each year at sunrise on 17 June to the top of Bunker's Hill and there beat the tune 'Yankee Doodle' on the drum made from Mr Sanborn's pelt: 'The drumheads

57

to be respectively inscribed with Pope's *Universal Prayer* and the Declaration of Independence, as originally worded by its illustrious author Thomas Jefferson.' The term 'red-neck' seems inadequate to describe a man who shed his entire epidermis in celebration of American nationhood.

Some people, even in the days when lavish funerals were common, exhibited a sturdy independence and opted for a do-it-yourself burial. One such was John Underwood, a citizen of Lexington, in America, who was buried at Wittesca on 6 May 1735. His will made provision for a funeral which attempted to recapture the stoicism of classical times. No bells were to be rung and none of his family were to attend; the bier was to be painted green and his body was to be dressed in his ordinary clothes; his head and shoulders were to be pillowed on copies of the works of Horace, those of Milton at his feet. A small Greek bible at his right hand made a perfunctory gesture to Christianity, on his left was yet another copy of Horace, inscribed in Latin: 'A friend to the Muses, J.U.'

His instructions were carried out exactly, and when the grave was filled in, the six friends who were the only permitted mourners sang a stanza from one of Horace's odes, before adjourning to the house of the deceased, whose sister, though barred from the funeral, then presided over an elaborate supper. After the meal another Horatian ode was sung and drinks were served. Mr Underwood's sister was left $50,000 in return for organizing the funeral as he had directed; each of his friends received the equivalent of £10 sterling, on condition they did not wear mourning. The final clause in the will of this American humanist read: 'I request my friends to separate, after drinking cheerfully together, and to think no more of John Underwood.'

 enerally speaking, though, the motive behind do-it-yourself burial instructions was good old-fashioned miserliness. The Rev. Luke Imber, J.P., of Christchurch in Hampshire, like his fellow-cleric, the Rev. Langton Freeman, pretended all his life to be poorer than he was. To keep up this image, he dressed like a pauper, although he had a good income. Mr Imber, however, did not deny himself those comforts of life which could be had free, as was demonstrated when, at the age of eighty-three, he married a girl of thirteen. Contrary to the expectations of his friends, he survived the challenge of this physically unequal match and died at the ripe old age of ninety. But the cautious clergyman did not allow this idyll in his twilight years to lull his sense of economy: in his will he asked to be buried in an old chest which he had set aside for the purpose, thus saving the expense of a coffin.

Daniel Martinett, who died at Calcutta, gave similar directions: 'As to this fulsome carcase having already seen enough of worldly pomp, I desire nothing relative to it to be done, only its being stowed away in my old green chest, to avoid expense; for as I lived profusely, I die frugally.' Yet, despite his prodigality of life-style, Mr Martinett had not entirely neglected to make certain basic provisions, since he then confided with evident satisfaction, 'The undertaker's fees come to nothing, as I won them from him at a game of billiards.'

On the other hand, Mrs Maria Redding, who died in 1870, did not grudge the cost of both a lead and an elm coffin, one within the other. But if she died away from home, she had a scheme to defray the expense of transporting her remains, which she set out in her will. She instructed that they were to be 'enclosed in a plain deal box, and conveyed by goods train to Poole. Let no mention be made of the contents, as the conveyance will then not be charged more for than an ordinary package'. Mrs Redding added the helpful tip that 'the easiest way to get the coffin out of the house will be to take out one of the dining-room windows', a puzzling provision, since she seems to have assumed that it would be carried *into* the house by the usual entrance.

Of course, if you wanted an example of the ultimate in

59

straightforward, no-nonsense, self-help burial, then you needed to look no further than the British aristocracy, even in the middle of Queen Victoria's circumspect, bourgeois reign. Thus, when Lady Truro died, her husband simply had a shallow grave dug in the lawn in front of the family seat at Falconhurst, where he himself laid his spouse to rest. This was done at her own request and she had personally selected the exact spot; she had also insisted on being buried in a flimsy box, so that her body would decay as quickly as possible.

. . . A shallow grave dug in the lawn.

Lie heavy on him, Earth! for he
Laid many heavy loads on thee!

So ran Abel Evans's witty epitaph on the great architect Sir John Vanbrugh. Yet a surprising number of testators seemed to want as heavy a mass as possible piled upon their inert remains. Sir James Tillie of Pentilly Castle in Cornwall, who died in 1712, desired to be buried under a tower which stood in his park, where he had often passed happy days with his friends. Another tower burial was requested sixty years later by Mr Hull, a bencher of the Inner Temple. The outsize tombstone under which he elected to lie was Leith Hill Tower, in Surrey, which he had built himself a few years before his death.

Even more picturesque was the request of Baskerville, the famous printer who gave his name to a variety of type, to be buried under a windmill close to his garden. But the desire for tall landmarks as gravestones did not stop there. When Lord Camelford, the famous duellist, died a natural death in 1804, a codicil to his will was found to give directions for his burial under the centre tree of a group of three which stood on the bank of the Lake of St Lampierre, in Switzerland. Unhappily, the Napoleonic War had broken out by then, so that this conflict of nations prevented his heirs from carrying out the wishes of a man who had engaged in so many single combats during his lifetime.

Sir Charles Hastings, Bart., who died in 1823, made a more positive contribution to arboriculture. His will directed that his body should be buried uncoffined, swathed only in a cloth of perishable material in the grounds of his house. Then the earth covering him was to be sown with acorns and the best resultant sapling carefully cultivated 'that after my death my body may not be entirely useless, but may serve to rear a good English oak'. He also left a small legacy to his gardener, 'to see that the plant is well watered, and kept free from weeds'. These orders were obeyed, except that the burial took place in the nearby churchyard, and in due course Sir Charles gave birth to a fine oak tree.

At the opposite extreme, Thomas Hollis of Corscombe, in Dorset, could not tolerate the weight of even the smallest memorial over his body. In his will he asked to be buried in any one of a group of fields close to his house, which was immediately to be ploughed up, so that no trace of his grave should remain. Mr Hollis, an early ecumenist who indiscriminately attended the Established and Dissenting churches as the mood took him, made it easy for his heirs to comply with his wishes: on New Year's Day, 1774, while giving orders to a workman in one of the fields designated in his will, he obligingly fell down and expired on the spot.

𝔄 recurring, morbid preoccupation among testators was the fear of being buried alive. Edgar Allan Poe's was not the only overactive imagination to dwell on this horrific possibility. The will of William Blackett, Governor of Plymouth, in 1782, asked 'that my body may be kept as long as it may not be offensive; and that one or more of my toes or fingers may be cut off, to secure a certainty of my being dead'. On the assumption that the test proved positive, he added in a different vein: 'I also make this request to my dear wife, that as she has been troubled with one old fool, she will not think of marrying a second.'

Nearly a century later, one John Louis Greftulke wrote a clause into his will refusing burial. His corpse was to be embalmed and placed in a coffin with a glass lid: 'also I desire it be not nailed down, so that my body may not be deprived of air and light. Ultimately it may be buried, if the law permit'.

The dread of premature burial has continued into the twentieth century. A woman who died in Kent several decades ago left large amounts to charity in her will, but instructed that 'my body shall be stabbed to the heart to make sure that life is extinct'. This safeguard was more drastic than Governor Blackett's scheme, since it protected the lady against suffocation, but doomed her in any case — another example of the superior subtlety of the eighteenth-century mind!

Until recently, of course, another major issue was cremation. The opposition of the churches to this means of disposal of human remains kindled a corresponding fanaticism among its supporters, who began to insert conditions in their wills to enforce their wishes. A pioneering example was Mrs Pratt, of Hanover Square, who made history on 26 September 1769, when the instructions in her will were 'punctually fulfilled by the burning of her body to ashes in her grave in the new burying-ground adjoining to Tyburn turnpike'.

More unselfish motives inspired William Kensett, who was convinced that graveyards full of mouldering corpses must spread disease. In the public interest, therefore, when he died in 1855 he left his corpse to the Imperial Gas Company in London, to be burned in one of their retorts. Although he thoughtfully supplied £10 to cover expenses, Mr Kensett added pessimistically:

> Should a defence of fanaticism and superstition prevent their granting this my request, then my executors must submit to have my remains buried, in the plainest manner possible, in my family grave in St John's Wood Cemetery, to assist in poisoning the living in that neighbourhood.

In the late nineteenth century, Sir Benjamin Richardson, a distinguished medical man, was also a champion of cremation. An old man who wanted to be cremated, against his daughter's wishes, called on him one day and asked him to be his executor. Richardson explained that this would make no difference, since the old man's daughter would still have the final say in the disposal of his body. He suggested instead that the old man should leave a large amount in his will to the society promoting cremation, only to be effective if his daughter refused to have his body burned. This was agreed and not long afterwards the elderly testator died. His son-in-law, a clergyman, then visited Sir Benjamin Richardson and told him that he would not allow a cremation. 'I'm jolly glad,' the famous doctor replied, 'for in that case my society will benefit to the extent of something like ten thousand pounds.' The dismayed curate went home to sleep on the problem and, next day, wrote to say that, since it would be even more sinful to help the society to such a windfall, he and his wife would reluctantly permit his father-in-law's cremation.

Nowadays cremation is commonplace, but the fertile minds of testators continue to enrich even this clinical process with colourful burial instructions amid the drabness of the late twentieth century. In America, a company called Astro Burials, based in Wyoming, recently investigated the possibility of scattering ashes in space, 'among the stars'. The ashes would go up on the space shuttle, when it becomes operative, and costs are estimated at about $4,000 compared with $3,000 for a normal burial. But the individual in recent years who most worthily picked up the torch, so to speak, of testamentary whimsy was surely Greta Pegg, who had served for thirty-six years as barmaid at Doncaster Greyhound Stadium. In accordance with her will, she was cremated and then, between races on a Saturday

Her ashes were scattered on to the dog track.

evening and with the spectators observing a respectful silence, her ashes were scattered from their urn on to the dog track beside which this faithful barmaid had herself poured many a jar. It is to be hoped that the assorted authors of similarly bizarre burial instructions — misers and snuff-takers, epicures and mummies — watched with ghostly approval this latest manifestation of a great tradition.

Malevolent Wills

ot all testators shared the honest purpose of Sir Francis Drake, that model of English chivalry, who, in 1595, desired 'to leave behinde me all thinges in a good and decent order, to th'intent noe controversie or discention shoulde after my decease arise or growe'. On the contrary, many have used their wills as instruments of revenge, a last opportunity for settling old scores from the security of the grave. Their motives have been as varied as the fanciful harassments they have dreamed up. Henpecked husbands lead the field — the largest number of malevolent wills are directed against wives — but plain malice or prejudice against certain individuals, religious beliefs, or even styles of dress have inspired a huge assortment of vindictive wills. *De mortuis nil nisi bonum* may be a binding maxim for the living, but the dead are untrammelled by any such Queensberry Rules and have regularly thumbed their noses at their surviving families and acquaintances through the malicious provisions of their last wills and testaments.

To be 'cut off with a shilling' was the traditional fate of an offending heir. The phrase is suitably stark: along with 'dead and never called me mother!' it is one of the great clichés of Victorian melodrama. In fact, the custom of bequeathing a shilling was a superstition based on laymen's ignorance of the law. Some countries did have rules which made a will invalid if the testator's heir was totally excluded, but this never applied in England when a man was disposing of his own property. Where the popular misunderstanding probably arose was in respect of those special cases where a person was exercising a delegated power to dispose of someone else's property

65

among several people; in such situations, every potential beneficiary had to receive at least a nominal share (e.g. one shilling), but even this restriction was abolished in 1874. Apart from the widely-believed fallacy that an heir must be left at least a shilling to make the will legal, however, it seems likely that the popularity of cutting people off with a shilling was largely due to vindictiveness: an heir who was completely overlooked might preserve some shabby dignity, but to receive a shilling made him ridiculous and advertised publicly the contempt in which the testator held him.

Embittered husbands, who, as has been mentioned, were most prominent among malevolent testators, frequently favoured this device. Sometimes they accompanied the bequest with a few explanatory remarks, like Mr John George, of Lambeth, who died in 1791, whose will contained the following observations regarding his wife:

> The strength of Samson, the genius of Homer, the prudence of Augustus, the skill of Pyrrhus, the patience of Job, the philosophy of Socrates, the subtlety of Hannibal, the vigilance of Hermogenes, would not suffice to subdue the perversity of her character . . . weighing maturely and seriously all these considerations, I have bequeathed, and I bequeath, to my said wife Elizabeth, the sum of one shilling, to be paid unto her within six months of my death.

Bitterness against wives, of course, was not confined to shilling wills. With the secure barrier of death between himself and his spouse's shrewish tongue or tyrannical rolling-pin, the most downtrodden of husbands could afford to avenge a lifetime of marital misery.

Early wills, against the general trend, often showed concern for the welfare of the testator's wife, like that of William Holybrande, a London tailor, who, in 1505, bequeathed £5 to his servant 'so that he be lovyng and gentill to my wyfe' — clearly a sixteenth-century Admirable Crichton! By a hundred years later, however, things had deteriorated. On 10 January 1608, William Pym, of Woolavington in Somerset, gave utterance to his grievances:

> I give to Agnes, which I did a long time take for my wyfe — till shee denyd me to be her husband, all though wee were marryd with my friends' consent, her father, mother, and uncle at it; and now she swareth she will neither love mee nor evyr bee perswaded to, by preechers, nor by any other, which hath happened within these few yeres. And Toby Andrewes, the beginner, which I did see with mine own eyes when hee did more than was fitting, and this by means of others their abettors. I have lived a miserable life this six or seven yeres, and now I leve the revenge to God — and tenn pounds to buy her a gret horse, for I could not this manny yeres plese her with one gret enough.

The description of Mr Toby Andrews as a 'beginner' would seem to carry a distinctive, seventeenth-century meaning.

The cuckolded William Pym was in good company, however, for rank was no protection against misfortune. Henry, 1st Earl of Stafford, loyally followed James II into exile in France, where he married the daughter of the notorious Comte de Grammont. She inherited her father's moral failings, so that the marriage was a disaster. Lord Stafford relieved his feelings in his will, published at his death in April 1719: 'To the worst of women, Claude Charlotte de Grammont, unfortunately my wife, guilty as she is of all crimes, I leave five-and-forty brass halfpence, which will buy a pullet for her supper.' Mutual accusations of crime were common between husbands and wives. In 1785, one Parker, a Bond Street bookseller, bequeathed 'to Elizabeth Parker, the sum of £50, whom, through my foolish fondness, I made my wife, without regard to family, fame, or fortune; and who, in return, has not spared, most unjustly, to accuse me of every crime regarding human nature, save highway-robbery'.

Three years later, another testator made a similar will, but with less generous financial provision: 'I, David Davis, of Clapham, Surrey, do give and bequeath to Mary Davis, daughter of Peter Delaport, the sum of five shillings, which is sufficient to enable her to get drunk for the last time at my expense'. In 1794, a kindred spirit, William Darley, of Ash in Hertfordshire, invoked the traditional penalty by leaving 'unto my wife, Mary Darley, for picking my pocket of 60 guineas, and taking up money in my name, of John Pugh, Esq., the sum of one shilling'. By the nineteenth century, jaundiced husbands were inventing refinements of cruelty, such as the man who left the respectable sum of 500 guineas to his wife, but stipulated that she was only to come into the enjoyment of it after her death, 'in order that she may be buried suitably as my widow'.

Often, however, the husband's motive was not revenge, but a desire to control his wife's behaviour after his death. Walter Frampton, Lord Mayor of Bristol, who died in 1838, thought it intolerable that any lesser mortal should step into the shoes of a high civic dignitary like himself. In his will, therefore, he left a large estate to his wife Isabella, but with the proviso that she must not remarry. If she did so, then his executors were ordered to strip her of the entire inheritance, 'making a triple proclamation of the same by sound of trumpet at the high cross'. An even more solemn public demonstration was demanded by Lieutenant-Colonel Nash, of Bath — possibly related to the famous Beau — who bequeathed an annuity to the town's bell-ringers to 'toll dolefully' on every anniversary of his wedding.

But more husbands were concerned, like Mayor Frampton, to preserve their memory and their dignity by employing the stick-and-carrot technique. The will of James Robbins, in 1869, gave his wife an incentive to wear mourning and not to remarry. 'In the event of my dear wife not complying with my request to wear a widow's cap after my decease, and in the event of her marrying again,' directed Mr Robbins, more in sorrow than in anger, 'then, and in both such cases, the annuity which shall be payable to her out of my estate shall be £20 per annum, and not £30.'

Husbands, however, were far from unanimous in approving widows' weeds. In complete contrast, a Mr Concauen insisted that his wife 'do not, after my decease, offend artistic taste, or blazon the sacred feelings of her sweet and gentle nature, by the exhibition of a widow's cap'. Another considerate testator, a landowner named Withipol, from Walthamstow, left his estate to his wife with the contrite prediction 'that she will marry no man, for fear to meet with so evil a husband as I have been to her'. Such death-bed remorse was unusual, though, and the prevailing spirit was typified by the Manchester man who disinherited his wife with the succinct observation, 'Many times she wished I was stiff.'

. . . His body to be boiled down and made into a candle.

In some instances the iron had entered into the testator's soul without the relationship having progressed as far as marriage. Disappointed lovers were prone to using their wills to get their own back on the women who had spurned them.

The most extravagant gesture of this kind was perpetrated by an acknowledged lunatic who, having lost his mind after being crossed in love, decided to commit suicide. First, however, he made his will, in which he ordered his body to be boiled down, the fat extracted and made into a candle. This, along with a letter enclosed in the will, was to be delivered at night time to the girl who had snuffed out his hopes, so that she could read his farewell message by his own light. This request was duly carried out, and it is to be hoped the lady found this last letter illuminating.

Since the worst quarrels usually occur within families, it is not surprising to find that when testators were not venting their spleen against their spouses, the next favourite target was their sons and heirs. Here is a cry from the heart, in an English gentleman's will of 1793:

I, Philip Thicknesse . . . leave my right hand, to be cut off after my death, to my son, Lord Audley; and I desire it may be sent to him, in hopes that such a sight may remind him of his duty to God, after having so long abandoned the duty he owed to a father who once affectionately loved him.

This macabre legacy may have proved a chastening experience for Lord Audley, but even disinheritance is relative, as one indignant father demonstrated. In his will, proved in 1810, Richard Crawshay, of Cyfartha in Glamorgan, who belonged to a family of industrialists well-known for their eccentricity, made this bequest: 'To my only son, who never would follow my advice, and has treated me rudely in very many instances; instead of making him my executor and residuary legatee (as till this day he was), I give him £100,000.' Well, it was better than being cut off with a shilling!

Some parents' wills, not necessarily of malevolent intent, imposed a responsibility upon their children which was either unwelcome or incapable of precise legal definition. Such a case occurred in 1970. Mrs Irene Andrews, who had died the previous year, left the income from more than 18,000 shares in the family furnishing business to her son Christopher, an estate agent. The condition attached to this legacy, however, was that he 'shall have adopted or shall adopt within two years of my death a coloured child to be brought up as one of his family'. Otherwise, the income was to be divided between Oxfam and Christian Aid. But the condition was declared void at Lancashire Chancery Court, in Manchester, on 21 July 1970. Giving his decision, Vice-Chancellor Thomas Burgess said, 'In my judgement I cannot determine with certainty what this testatrix indicated by the use of the words "coloured child".' So Mr Andrews was free to receive his legacy without fulfilling the adoption requirements. It is perhaps worth recording that his address, as given in court, was in Sussex — in the village of Blackboys!

More comprehensively, a nineteenth-century Canadian worthy called Dr Dunlop took advantage of his will to catalogue the inadequacies of his entire family. He bequeathed his five-acre field to his eldest sister 'to console her for being married to a man she is obliged to henpeck', and the adjoining cottage to his second sister 'because as no one is likely to marry her it will be large enough to lodge her'. One of his brothers was left 'my big silver watch, that he may know the hour at which men ought to rise from their beds'; a brother-in-law received 'my best pipe, out of gratitude that he married my sister Maggie whom no man of taste would have taken'; and a friend was given 'a silver teapot, that, being afflicted with a slatternly wife, he may therefrom drink tea to his comfort'. It is not difficult to imagine how lively an occasion the reading of this will must have been.

Malevolence directed against the testator's whole family seems to have been a North American foible.

Another example was the last will and testament of Dr Everett Wagner, a miser, of Barksville, Kentucky, dated 1 March 1888. After describing how his family, who had always previously shunned him, had all visited him during his last illness and hinted that they would each like to have a trinket of some kind as a memento of him, Dr Wagner declared, 'On account of their former treatment and their quiet hints, I now take this method of satisfying their desire'. There then followed a series of bequests, beginning with: 'To my beloved brother

. . . And to his brothers, his right and left legs and feet.

Napoleon Bonaparte Wagner my left hand and arm'; another brother, George Washington Wagner, was presented with his right hand and arm; his two remaining brothers received respectively his right and left legs and feet. To his nephew, C. H. Hatfield, he bequeathed his nose; to his nieces, Hettie and Clara, an ear each; his less favoured cousins were only given his teeth and gums. 'It grieves me to have to part with myself in this manner, but then,' observed Dr Wagner stoically, 'what is a gift without a sacrifice?' He set aside $1,000 to cover the cost of dissecting his body, while the remainder of his $12,000 estate went to public charities. As a courteous after-thought, a codicil dated two days later assigned 'to my beloved sister-in-law Mrs C. G. Wagner my liver'.

72

𝔓robably the most comprehensively malicious will of all time was that of Philip, 4th Earl of Pembroke, who died on 23 January 1650. It was more a manifesto than a testament and it reflected the bitterness which had been created by the only civil war in English history. After rehearsing some of the historic events he had witnessed — 'I well remember me that five years ago I did give my vote for the despatching of old Canterbury, neither have I forgotten that I did see my King upon the scaffold' — Lord Pembroke gave instructions for his burial. 'Above all,' he adjured his executors, 'put not my body beneath the church-porch, for I am, after all, a man of birth, and I would not that I should be interred there, where Colonel Pride was born.' (This was a reference to the Cromwellian officer who had 'purged' Parliament.) He then bequeathed most of his horses to Lord Fairfax, 'that when Cromwell and his council take away his commission he may still have some *horse* to command'. To the Earl of Salisbury he left his menagerie of wild beasts, 'being very sure he will preserve them, seeing that he refused the King a doe out of his park'. Next, he presented his chaplains to the Earl of Stamford, who had never employed any, apart from his own son, Lord Grey, 'who, being at the same time spiritual and carnal, will engender more than one monster'.

From these sarcastic beginnings, Lord Pembroke went on to indulge in an orgy of aristocratic bitchiness.

Item: I give *nothing* to my Lord Saye, and I do make him this legacy willingly, because I know that he will faithfully distribute it unto the poor. Item: Seeing that I did menace a certain Henry Mildmay, but did not thrash him, I do leave the sum of fifty pounds sterling to the lacquey that shall pay unto him my debt. Item: I bequeath to Thomas May, whose nose I did break at a mascarade, five shillings. My intention had been to give him more; but all who shall have seen his *History of the Parliament* will consider that even this sum is too large.

And so, clause by clause, his lordship blasted the members of the Cromwellian establishment. He saved his heaviest salvo until near the end, however, when he turned his guns on the biggest target of all: 'Item: I give to the Lieutenant-General Cromwell one of my words, the which he must want, seeing that he hath never kept any of his own'.

With the nobility giving so waspish a lead, humbler folk were not slow to follow. A will of 1770 read: 'I, Stephen Swain, of the parish of St Olave, Southwark, give to John Abbot, and Mary, his wife, sixpence each, to buy for each of them a halter, for fear the sheriffs should not be provided'. In 1781, Mr John Hylett Stow directed his executors to spend five guineas in buying 'a picture of the viper biting the benevolent hand of the person who saved him from perishing in the snow', and present it to a certain King's Counsel who might contemplate it and ponder which was more profitable — 'a grateful remembrance of past friendship and almost parental regard, or ingratitude and insolence'. The indignant testator added that this was 'in lieu of a legacy of three thousand pounds I had by a former will, now revoked and burned, left him'.

On the continent, the malevolent will was as popular an institution as in Britain. A crotchety old German professor, for example, who died in Berlin in the early nineteenth century, loathed his only surviving relative. So he devised a revenge that was characteristically Teutonic in its attention to basics. He left all his property to his heir, but on condition he should wear white linen clothes at all seasons; if he put on extra underclothes in winter, he was to forfeit his inheritance.

Contrastingly, in France, the millionaire Marquis d'Aligre, who died in 1847, displayed a spirit of Gallic frivolity. 'I leave 200,000 francs a year,' he announced, 'to the "Phalansterians" ' (a commune-dwelling sect of socialist visionaries); 'but they are only to receive this sum on the day on which they shall have transformed the ocean into orangeade, and gratified mankind with that appendage he needs to make him equal to the gibbon.'

It might be expected that lawyers at least would be immune from the temptation to pervert a solemn legal document into a litany of hate: not so, as witness the will of a somewhat paranoid barrister. 'I leave to Herbert L—, his wife, and Frances Elizabeth, my sister,' he snarled, 'the happy assurance that their greed, jealousy, folly, plots, schemes, and vile lies have succeeded in making life a burden to me.'

Nor has the tendency to pay off old scores in wills abated in modern times. Mr Wilfred Mee, a Leicestershire bachelor, who died in March 1972, had quarrelled perpetually with his neighbours during his lifetime. In his will, therefore, as an intended annoyance to them, he gave instructions that an Indian or Pakistani should be offered first refusal of his cottage at Mountsorrel. But Mr Mee's plan was frustrated by the fact that no Indians or Pakistanis were interested in buying his house, which was sold instead to a young English couple. Mr Mee's next-door neighbour, who described him as 'the most cantankerous person I have ever met in my life', said that in any case he would have had no objection to coloured neighbours, adding candidly, 'I should have preferred an Eskimo to Mr Mee.'

Some malevolent wills, of course, were little more than the expression of an idiosyncratic sense of humour. Jasper Mayne, who died in 1620, bequeathed to his valet a battered portmanteau which contained, as he promised in his will, something that would make him drink. The excited servant tore open the trunk, only to discover that its sole content was a red herring!

A primary motive in making wills, however, was to prolong the testator's influence beyond his death, in order to discourage or suppress certain habits among his heirs. Centuries ago, a French landowner, the Seigneur de la Tour-Oliergues, put a clause in his will restricting his third son to a life income of forty livres, because he was a vegetarian, and he has had many imitators since.

The twentieth-century controversy over smoking is actually an old issue, as a succession of wills can illustrate. Peter Campbell, a Derbyshire gentleman, made his will on 20 October 1616, in which he left all his household effects to his son Roger. But there was a condition 'that yf at any time hereafter, any of his brothers or sisters' (there were eight of them) 'shall fynd him

'. . . Any of his brothers or sisters finding him taking of tobacco, shall have the said goods . . .'

takeing of tobacco, that then he or she so fynding him, and making just prooffe thereof to my executors, shall have the said goods . . .'

More than two hundred years later, in America, the original home of the noxious weed, a Maine farmer insisted that any of his descendants, 'born or yet unborn,' who should be found smoking, chewing tobacco, or drinking alcohol — unless prescribed by a physician under oath — should be 'cut off from their dower in my property for six months for the first offence, and one year for each subsequent offence; and for one year of total abstinence, his or their dowers to be restored'. A codicil extended the prohibition to gambling.

It is understandable that parents and guardians should have been concerned about their heirs smoking or gaming. Less rational was the crusade against moustaches. Herr Bechtel, for example, a nineteenth-century testator in Germany, excluded from a share in his estate any of his

'... Excluding any male descendants wearing a moustache.'

male descendants who should persist in wearing a moustache. (This was one prejudice that would not have been countenanced under the Third Reich!)

In England, the will of Henry Budd, proved in 1862, left his estates of Pepper Park and Twickenham Park respectively to his sons Edward and William. If either of them wore a moustache, however, then his share also would accrue to his clean-shaven brother. Just seven years later, a Pimlico upholsterer called Fleming bequeathed £10 each to all the men in his employment, but in the cases of those continuing to flaunt a moustache, the legacy was reduced to £5.

77

Many wills sought to enforce moral standards on heirs. The Victorian testament of Mr J. Sargeant, of Leicester, required his nephews to prove to his executors that they had risen from bed and either occupied themselves with business or taken open-air exercise 'from five to eight o'clock every morning from the 5th of April to the 10th of October, being three hours each day, and from seven to nine o'clock in the morning from the 10th of October to the 5th of April, being two hours every morning . . .' This régime was to be followed for seven years, otherwise his nephews forfeited all share in his estate. 'Temperance makes the faculties clear, and exercise makes them vigorous,' observed Mr Sargeant. 'It is temperance and exercise that can alone ensure the fittest state for mental or bodily exertion.'

A similar spirit of cold-shower morality animated a Yorkshire rector who died in 1804. He left his large property to his daughter, but forbade her to marry without the permission of his executors. A further clause imposed upon her the standard of modesty that would make her an eligible bride for an English gentleman:

> Seeing that my daughter Anna has not availed herself of my advice touching the objectionable practice of going about with her arms bare up to the elbows, my will is that, should she continue after my death in this violation of the modesty of her sex, all the goods, chattels, moneys, land, and other that I have devised to her for the maintenance of her future life shall pass to the oldest of the sons of my sister Caroline.

The reverend gentleman was aware, however, that people of more permissive outlook might belittle his fears that the red-blooded youth of Yorkshire would find their passions inflamed by the sight of a nude female forearm. 'Should anyone take exception to this my wish as being too severe,' he concluded firmly, 'I answer that licence in dress in a woman is a mark of a depraved mind.'

Concern for female virtue has continued to preoccupy testators up to the present day. The advance of women's liberation seems to have made little impression upon Mr Philip Eswyth Grundy, a dentist from Leyland in Lancashire, who died in November, 1973. When his will was published on 15 March 1974, it transpired that he had left the bulk of his £181,841 estate to his nurse, provided she refrained from wearing cosmetics or going out with men for a period of five years. Mr Grundy's directions were meticulous; the fortunate heiress must 'never use any lipstick or any other make-up of any kind whatsoever apart from clear nail varnish, and wear no jewellery such as rings, earrings, necklaces, and never go out with any men on her own, or with a party of men, during the five years'. The strait-laced attitudes of *Mrs* Grundy have long been proverbial; this will suggests that the male of the species is no less illiberal.

Inevitably, vindictiveness in wills was often directed against particular races or religions. Anti-Irish feeling was common among English testators, but few of them made so significant a gesture as Jonathan Swift, himself a very distinguished Irishman, who donated most of his estate for the founding of an Irish lunatic asylum:

Proving by one satiric touch
No nation needed it so much.

Later in the eighteenth century, an Englishman, who had always detested the Irish, inherited a property in Tipperary, on condition he resided there. Unfortunately, in this case familiarity only bred deeper contempt, so that, by the time of his death on 17 March (ironically, St Patrick's Day!) 1791, his hatred for all things Irish had become pathological. Thus, feeling himself to have been the victim of a malicious will, he in turn used his last testament as an instrument of revenge. In it he left £10 annually for the purchase of a large quantity of whiskey, to be distributed among not more than twenty Irishmen who were to assemble in the graveyard where he was

79

buried, on every anniversary of his death. The whiskey was to be served in half-pint measures and each Irishman was to be provided with a stout oaken stick and a knife. It was the testator's fond hope that the annual massacre provoked by these thoughtful dispositions would eventually eradicate the Irish race from the neighbourhood, which might then 'be colonised by civilised and respectable Englishmen'.

Another prevailing sentiment in Anglo-Saxon wills was dislike of Catholicism. A classic example was that of the Hon. Mrs Araminta Monck Ridley (a peculiarly schizophrenic name for a Protestant zealot), proved in 1869, which decreed: 'That if any or either of my said children, either in my lifetime or at any time after my decease, shall become or shall marry a Roman Catholic, or shall join or enter any Ritualistic brotherhood or sisterhood,' then the legacies to them were to become void.

From time to time, judges have tried to fire a warning shot across the bows of malevolent testators. For example, a Scottish widow who died in 1934 left a very controversial holograph will, in which she bequeathed to certain relatives of her dead husband the sum of one farthing each 'as a reward for their mean scheming for years' — the Scots are a frugal race and the traditional shilling would probably have seemed extravagant. A marginal note denounced one of these farthing legatees as 'that dangerous intriguing female, that Arch schemer! She wanted to compel me to buy her old hats at a £1 each.' She then went on to make an accusation of fraud against a Glasgow solicitor who had been involved in winding-up her husband's estate. These defamatory statements led to legal action in the Court of Session in Scotland and, in the course of his judgement, on 21 June 1935, the Lord Justice-Clerk said: 'If people who are minded to use their wills to slander other people . . . realize that they run a grave risk that their estates may be depleted by claims of damages arising out of the slander, and their testamentary intentions may thereby be defeated, it may exercise a salutary restraint upon this most objectionable form of malice.' Alas! The heirs of the Marquis d'Aligre had as much hope of accomplishing their task of turning the ocean into orangeade as the judiciary had of deterring testators from venting their spleen. Just eight years later, in 1943, an English judge had to order the words 'for the family honour' to be excluded from probate of a woman's will, on the grounds that they suggested dishonourable conduct by a person named in the text.

And so it continues. Downtrodden husbands, rigid moralists, women scorned, and people who need no motive beyond their own truculence — all plot secret vengeance for real or imagined wrongs. Signed, sealed and secure, their wills repose unsuspected during their lifetime in a lawyer's safe, like time-bombs set to explode immediately after their deaths. There is no more implacable judge of his fellow men than the malevolent testator; he is invulnerable in his self-righteousness.

Sir William Petty, who died in 1687, epitomized the will-maker's sturdy indifference to public opinion, when he condemned bequests to charities:

> As for legacies for the poor, I am at a stand; as for beggars by trade and election, I give them nothing; as for impotents by the hand of God, the publick ought to maintain them; as for those who have been bred to no calling nor estate, they should be put upon their kindred . . . as for those who compassionate the sufferings of any object, let them relieve themselves by relieving such sufferers.

Well, it was all good, downright, homespun philosophy, but precious little joy for the Battersea Dogs' Home!

'And as regards my Pussies ...'

So many testators have been animal-lovers that dog and cat homes — and, more recently, such specialized institutions as donkey sanctuaries — have been the recipients of a huge number of legacies. But not every will-maker is satisfied with such generalized charity; many have been moved to make a more personal gesture towards an individual animal who, they felt, had a claim on their bounty. As a result, domestic pets of every description have sometimes been bemused to discover that their late owners had made provision for them on a scale that would turn the head of the most phlegmatic ginger-tom or Labrador.

Cats have an especial gift for ingratiating themselves with their masters or mistresses, and this talent has raised many a feline opportunist from a precarious living as a subsistence mouser to cushioned luxury and a diet of smoked salmon. This is nothing new. A seventeenth-century German Jesuit called Jeremias Drexel, one of whose works was translated into English under the cheerful title *The Forerunner of Eternity, or Messenger of Death sent to healthy, sick, and dying Men,* recorded the case of a woman who left 500 gold pieces in her will to her cats, 'so that they might always enjoy a good table'.

In France, Madame Dupuis, a celebrated harpist who died in 1677, inserted the following clause into her otherwise violently malevolent will: 'Item. I desire my sister, Marie Bluteau, and my niece, Madame Calonge, to look to my cats. If both should survive me, thirty sous a week must be laid out upon them, in order that they may live well.' She then added meticulous dietary instructions. The cats were to be served daily 'in a clean and proper manner' with two meals of meat-soup, the same as was eaten by the household, in two separate plates; the bread was not to be broken up into the soup, but divided into squares the size of a nut, 'otherwise they will refuse to eat it'. Finely minced meat was to be added, then the meal was to be seasoned and simmered in a clean pan before being served. The testatrix's niece was also required to visit the cats three times a week.

Miss Charlotte Rosa Raine, of St Margaret's Lodge, Woodstock, Oxfordshire, died on 19 June 1894, and her will was proved on 28 August following. Among other idiosyncratic bequests, she left her lands and hereditaments in the parish of Wolvercote, near Oxford, to Lord Randolph Churchill 'in recognition of his commanding political genius'. Unfortunately, it appears that the distinguished statesman turned down this windfall. Miss Raine, however, quickly pressed on to more serious matters. 'And as regards my pussies,' her will continued, her dear old white puss Titiens and her pussies Tabby Rolla, Tabby Jennefee, and black-and-white Ursula were left to Ann Elizabeth Matthews, who was to receive £12 a year for the upkeep of each cat so long as it lived. Louise and Dr Clausman (both cats) were to go to Elizabeth Willoughby (her maid); her Black Ebony and White Oscar were to become the property of Miss Lavinia Sophia Beck. Both these beneficiaries were also to receive £12 a year per cat. 'All the remainder of my pussies,' were additionally bequeathed to Ann Elizabeth Matthews, and the executors were ordered to pay her £150 a year out of the dividends of the testatrix's father's shares in Lambeth Waterworks towards their support, but, Miss Raine stipulated, 'this is not to extend to kittens afterwards born'. Ann Elizabeth Matthews (happy heiress!) was further directed to live off this annuity in a cottage and garden for the maintenance of the same pussies, 'unless the Rev. William Martin Spencer is willing to permit the pussies to reside on the premises and in the garden at Pound'.

84

Miss Raine's will, made at the height of Victorian affluence, illustrates the rising expectations of cats. But even the decline of the human economy has not reversed their fortunes; on the contrary, it is in the twentieth century that feline beneficiaries have really come into their own, with the law formally vindicating their rights of inheritance in several notable cases. For example, Mr William Joseph Haines, of Long Buckby in Northamptonshire, expressed a wish in his will that his two cats should be provided for after his death. The trust in favour of the cats was tested in the Chancery Division on 6 November 1952, before Mr Justice Danckwerts. Counsel for the executors explained that, as the cats were not separately represented in court, he would have to argue on their behalf. Although the question might seem trivial, he was told that whereas it cost 7s 6d a week to keep a cat at home, it cost 17s 6d if it was boarded out. The following exchange then took place between the Bench and learned counsel.

His Lordship: 'It depends on the appetite of the cats.'
Counsel: 'Or whether they are good mousers.'
His Lordship: 'Is there any trouble with regard to the rule against perpetuities? How old are the cats?' Since counsel did not know, the judge then asked: 'Can I take judicial notice of the fact that sixteen years is a long life for any cat?'
Counsel: 'Yes, I think that you can.'

So Mr Justice Danckwerts ruled that the executors were entitled to provide for the maintenance of the two cats.

American cats have prospered too. Mrs Alma Culbert, who died in 1958, left $23,000 to her cat, as sole beneficiary of her will, proved at St Petersburgh, Florida. Rastus and Lucy, two sophisticat(e)s from Seattle, inherited their owner's family home, with a housekeeper and maid to attend to their wants and a trust to ensure their financial security. As lately as 1975, however, legal experts predicted that the law would not uphold the will

85

of Mr Robert Weiss, who bequeathed his $8,000 estate to his appropriately named pet, Kat. The beneficiary, a brown-and-white tabby, had cause to purr when the will was successfully proved at San José, California, on 12 March 1975.

These examples would seem to demonstrate that cats have done pretty well in the testamentary stakes, but not everyone thought so. Mrs Mary Barnes, from Bath, who died at the age of eighty-six in January 1968, believed that cats were often neglected. She therefore willed both her houses to the Bath branch of the Royal Society for the Prevention of Cruelty to Animals, 'for the benefit of cats', and left estate worth £29,388 (after duty) for the same purpose. 'I am of the opinion that dogs generally have the sympathy of the public at large,' she explained in her will, 'and it is not generally appreciated that the welfare of cats can be overlooked.'

Although Mrs Barnes was unashamedly partisan in her championship of cats, she was correct in thinking that dogs held a very powerful place in the affections of testators. Men of distinction were prominent among their benefactors, even centuries ago when, for example, Dr Cristiano, an eminent European jurist, bequeathed 6,000 florins for the maintenance of his three dogs.

It was also notorious that dogs enjoyed protection in the highest quarters. The 1st Earl of Eldon, a former Lord Chancellor of England, left his dog Pincher to his younger daughter, Lady Frances Bankes, with an annuity of £8 to support him; unfortunately, Lady Frances outlived her father by little more than six months. Pincher, however, was a dog of such distinction that he was well cared for during the rest of his days. In his mature years, Pincher was generally held to bear a striking resemblance to Lord Eldon, particularly when he (the Earl) wore a wig. He was one of the most frequently painted dogs in England and, after Eldon's death in 1838, when Pincher survived to become a canine eminent Victorian, his portrait was executed by Landseer, who observed, 'He is a very picturesque old dog, with a wonderful look of cleverness in his face.'

Another distinguished testator was Sir James South, the founder-president of the Royal Astronomical Society, whose will was proved in 1868. In it, he bequeathed a pocket-watch each to the Earl of Shaftesbury, the Earl of Rosse, and Mr A. J. Stephens, on condition the watch was carried in the fob-pocket of the pantaloons, as was the testator's own usage, rather than in the waistcoat. Sir James also left £30 a year to a maidservant to look after Tiger, his favourite toy terrier. Four years later, the dog's existence was questioned, and Tiger had to appear in person in the Equity Court. His lawyer asked for a sum of £1,000 Consols to be set apart to meet the annuity, but the Vice-Chancellor regrettably held that the court's rules applied only to human beings. Tiger's continued security was guaranteed, however, by the executor's personal undertaking to the court for the remainder of the dog's life.

About the same time, confusion arose over the similar bequest made by a Mr Thomas Edmett. In a codicil to his will, made in 1861, he wrote: 'I bequeath to my faithful servant Elizabeth Osborne, on condition that she take care of my favourite dog, an annuity of £50 for her life, to be paid to her quarterly.' Now, at the time this will was made, the testator had a favourite dog called Romp; but Romp died before his master, who then acquired another dog called Sambo, which then became his favourite. So, at the time of Mr Edmett's death, in October 1871, the term 'my favourite dog' apparently applied to Sambo. The servant, Elizabeth Osborne, therefore, took Sambo into her care and claimed the £50 annuity. But the Vice-Chancellor ruled that she was entitled to the annuity in any case, since it was not her fault that Romp was not available to be cossetted by her; he urged her to cherish Sambo, but did not make the annuity conditional on this. And so they lived happily ever after (except, of course, for

Romp and Mr Edmett).

Jf American testators have been generous to cats, as already noted, they have been even more lavish in providing for dogs. A lawsuit was heard in the United States in 1947, arising out of the will of an attorney who had left his $30,000 estate to his two dogs, Pat and Gunner. The testator explained that the dogs could talk to him, that they enjoyed Mickey Mouse, and had well-defined tastes in literature. This tribute to the catholic culture of Pat and Gunner, however, cut no ice with the testator's disinherited brother, who contested the will. In the course of the trial, which lasted for three weeks, the two dogs were brought into court to exhibit the qualities which had endeared them to their late master. Unhappily for their cause, Pat and Gunner, presumably resentful of this indignity, refused to give any demonstration of their cultivated minds; instead, they growled sullenly at the Bench throughout their appearance. The impression which this created was fatal to their interests: the judge held that the testator had not been of sound mind, so that Pat and Gunner left the court $30,000 poorer, but with their self-respect uncompromised.

In an even more spectacular gesture, in 1959, Mrs Amy Roger Bachman, a San Francisco millionairess, left more than $600,000 to establish a memorial fund for her deceased terrier Bingo; her husband received $1. The memorial fund was to be administered by the San Francisco Society for the Prevention of Cruelty to Animals, and bequests to other charities amounted to $336,000. Mrs Bachman's son, who was left nothing at all, said: 'She had what I would call an extremely abnormal personality. I think she always preferred animals to people.'

Although a much smaller sum of money was involved, there was a similar case of testamentary discrimination in favour of a dog, at the expense of a husband, in

England in 1968. Mrs Iris Pothecary, of Highcliffe, near Bournemouth, willed £2,100 to Nimbus, her black-and-tan Alsatian, but nothing to her husband. Nimbus himself was left to a friend, with a bequest of £16 every month for looking after him, as well as a further sum of £100 to cover the cost of erecting a six-foot fence around the garden to keep him in. The will stated that if Nimbus died of old age or natural causes before the money was used up, the remainder should go to his new owner; but if he died through carelessness or was run over or lost, the balance should be divided equally between the Battersea Dogs' Home and the People's Dispensary for Sick Animals.

Probably, though, the British dog who most sensationally landed on his paws as a result of testamentary generosity was Sherry, a cairn terrier from Cheshire. (Terriers seem to have a knack of ingratiating themselves with rich testators — a quite disproportionate number of canine beneficiaries have belonged to this breed.) Sherry's owner bequeathed him more than £30,000, the income from which enabled him to live as the four-legged equivalent of a pools winner. Among the amenities which surrounded him was a heated kennel with running water

'. . . A heated kennel with running water and a fitted carpet.'

and a fitted carpet. On hearing the contents of the will, Sherry's kennel-maid said of him: 'I think he's my favourite of all the dogs. And I'm not just saying that because he's rich.'

Some testators conferred largesse on more than one species of animal. The Rt Hon. Humphry Morice, Member of Parliament for Launceston in the eighteenth century, held the impressive titles of Privy Councillor, Comptroller of the Household to George III, Lord Warden of the Stannaries, High Steward of the Duchy of Cornwall, and Rider and Master of the Forest of Dartmoor. The last title was the most deserved, for he was fanatically attached to horses and dogs. According to a contemporary, 'The honours shown by Mr Morice to his beasts of burthen were only inferior to those which Caligula lavished on his charger.'

In a codicil to his will, dated at Nice, 10 October 1782, he made generous provision for the occupants of his stables and kennels. The codicil took the form of a letter to William Burrell, one of his trustees, and directed him breathlessly:

> You and my other trustee are to receive £600 a year from my estates in Devon and Cornwall to pay for the maintenance of the horses and dogs I leave behind me and for the expense of servants to look after them besides Will Bishop the Groom he is I am persuaded very honest and will not let Bills be brought in for any oats hay straw or tares more than have really been had.

About thirty horses and dogs were provided for by this clause, some of whom survived their benefactor by a quarter of a century. Morice himself was slightly self-conscious about these arrangements for the animals, and later in the letter he confided, 'I thought it better to make my intention known to you by a private Letter as their being mentioned in my will would perhaps be ridiculed after my death and though I should be ignorant of it and of course not care about it yet the friends I leave behind me might not like to hear it.'

90

A smaller, but more varied menagerie featured in the will of a Mr Garland, in June 1828:

I bequeath to my monkey, my dear and amusing Jacko, the sum of ten pounds sterling per annum, to be employed for his sole and exclusive use and benefit; to my faithful dog Shock, and my well-beloved cat Tib, a pension of five pounds sterling; and I desire that, in case of the death of either of the three, the lapsed pension shall pass to the other two, between whom it is to be equally divided. On the death of all the three the sum appropriated to this purpose shall become the property of my daughter Gertrude, to whom I give this preference among my children because of the large family she has, and the difficulty she finds in bringing them up.

Again, the will of Mrs Elizabeth Balls, of Park Lodge, Streatham, proved on 5 November 1875, showed concern for animals. After bequests to various hospitals and charitable institutions amounting to £5,500 Consols — which more single-minded animal-loving testators would have deplored as crass sentimentality towards undeserving two-legged beneficiaries — Mrs Balls turned her attention to her late husband's cob mare and greyhound. The mare was to be kept in a comfortable, warm loosebox, as she had been since her master's death; she was not to be put to work, either in or out of harness, and her back was not to be crossed by any member of Mr Balls's family (evidently a corpulent race), but she was to be ridden by a person of light weight, at walking pace for not more than an hour, on four days a week at the most. The financial provision for the mare was £65 a year; the greyhound received an annuity of £5.

It may be noted in passing that, just as terriers as a breed have proved to be the favourites of testators, among horses the cob has most frequently benefited from wills. The French peasantry, for example, are not distinguished by their tender-heartedness towards animals, yet a rich countryman from near Toulouse stated in his will, in

1781: 'I declare that I appoint my russet cob my universal heir, and I desire that he may belong to my nephew George.' Although the will was contested, the royal courts upheld it — a typically urbane gesture by the Old Régime, just eight years before the French Revolution.

'. . . A typically urbane gesture by the Old Régime, just eight years before the French Revolution.'

Many less serviceable pets than horses and dogs were also testamentary beneficiaries. In 1813, a London woman began her will in this style: 'I, Elizabeth Orby Hunter, of Upper Seymour Street, widow, do give and bequeath to my beloved parrot, the faithful companion of 25 years, an annuity for its life of 200 guineas a year . . .' Mrs Hunter then went on to lay down elaborate precautions for establishing the parrot's identity, lest an impostor might be substituted, and measures for recovering the annuity from 'whoever could be base enough to do so'. The chosen custodian of the parrot — a Mrs Dyer — was also given 'the power to will and bequeath my parrot and its annuity to whomsoever she

92

pleases, provided that person is neither a servant nor a man — it must be bequeathed to some respectable female'. If this clause seems discriminatory, it must be borne in mind that parrots are notoriously corruptible: the slightest relaxation of moral vigilance and they will succumb to depravity. In a word (and that is the nub of the matter), exposure to the lower orders or to exclusively male society — notably that of seafarers — can provoke an irreversible deterioration in a parrot's vocabulary. So Mrs Hunter was only doing her duty as a responsible guardian.

Her further directions provided for suitable accommodation and protection from undesirable foreign influences: 'And I also will and desire, that 20 guineas may be paid to Mrs Dyer directly on my death, to be expended on a very high, long, and large cage for the foresaid parrot. It is also my will and desire, that my parrot shall not be removed out of England.' A final clause hinted delicately that Mrs Hunter had not found the rest of the world as sympathetic as her beloved parrot: 'Many owe to me both gratitude and money, but none have paid me either.'

But it was, as ever, the aristocracy who provided the most extravagant example of eccentricity. The Count of Mirandola, who lived at Lucca, acquired a pet carp in 1805, to which he became warmly attached. When he died, therefore, in 1825, he left a large annuity to the fish, along with elaborate instructions for its welfare. The carp was housed in a beautiful antique piscina, shaded by tropical plants, built on to the drawing-room of its master's villa, where it survived for more than ten years. With the insouciance of his class, however, the Count disdained to order any precautions against impersonation of his carp, as Mrs Hunter had done for her parrot.

The infatuation of the Count of Mirandola illustrates the phenomenon that those creatures which captivate testators are not necessarily drawn from the most companionable or demonstrative of species. More recently, in 1957, Mrs Emily Wilson, of Doncaster, bequeathed to her maidservant 'my tortoise, in the firm belief that she will look after and maintain the same'. To this end, Mrs Wilson also left her maid £100 for the upkeep of the tortoise; an identical sum went to the vicar and churchwardens of St George's parish church, Doncaster, in aid of the fabric repair fund.

Of course, will-makers who provide exclusively for their own domestic pets are open to the charge of self-indulgence. A form of animal benefaction, therefore, that has found wider social acceptance is the endowment of institutions, most often cat or dog homes. This type of bequest became popular in the nineteenth century and was regarded as more respectable than providing an isolated, sybaritic existence for a solitary parrot or carp.

Even here, however, there was room for idiosyncrasy. An American testator, Mr Jonathan Jackson, of Columbus, Ohio, who died last century, instructed his executors to build a home for cats, the plans for which he had drawn up in great detail. The building was to be equipped with dormitories, a refectory, and playing-fields. Other amenities were to include roofs that did not slope too steeply, so that they could be climbed easily, well-stocked rat-holes to provide sport, and a concert-hall where the cats were to listen to accordion music for an hour every day. Add to all this (as Mr Jackson's plans did) a sanatorium staffed by a veterinary surgeon and several trained nurses, and the whole grandiose scheme amounted to the world's first public school for cats. In his capacity as a feline Dr Arnold, Mr Jackson outlined his philosophy in his will: 'It is man's duty as lord of animals to watch over and protect the lesser and feebler, even as God watches over and protects man.'

Not every will, however, was good news for the testator's four-footed dependents. Miss Frances Pinckney, described as 'a veteran campaigner for the welfare of animals in Hampshire', who died on Christmas

Day, 1967, left a rather controversial will behind her. It decreed the humane killing of three donkeys and a pony belonging to her, after her death. Despite efforts to save the animals, they were destroyed by a veterinary surgeon two days later, at the deceased's cottage at Brockenhurst, near Bournemouth. Afterwards, the vet defended Miss Pinckney's decision, saying: 'She was a very practical woman who loved animals, and she knew that any other home would not have been as good as hers.'

But Miss Pinckney's will at least had the intention of looking after the animals' best interests, however drastic the method employed. Other wills have not been so well-intentioned. George Staverton, for example, who made his will in May 1661, left £6 a year for the purchase of a bull to be baited as sport by the poor of Wokingham, in Berkshire. The design was philanthropic and the proceeds from sale of the animal's hide and offal were to be used to buy shoes and stockings for pauper children. The bull-baiting took place annually in Wokingham market-place on 21 December until 1823, when the Corporation decided to end it.

Another bequest, which must have provoked equal irritation among human beings and animals, was contained in the will of John Rudge, dated 17 April 1725. Alongside various charitable donations, Mr Rudge gave five shillings quarterly to the parish of Trysull, Staffordshire, to pay a poor man to go round the church during sermons, waking up worshippers and driving out dogs. So, to redress the balance, it is perhaps worth remembering that while the fortunate pets of eighteenth-century benefactors like Humphry Morice luxuriated in their inheritances, the canine population of places like Trysull was denied freedom of conscience!

Bequests to dumb animals, of course, are only the tip of the iceberg, as regards curious legacies. Often the curiosity lay in the purpose to which the money was dedicated. A common object of bequests was the endowment of commemorative sermons, in England usually in thanksgiving for preservation from foreign invasion or Popery. Robert Wilcox, of Alcester in Warwickshire, by his will dated 24 December 1627, bequeathed a house and close to the town for the support of three annual sermons:

One upon the 5th of November, in remembrance of our happy deliverance, with our King, Nobles, and States, from the pestilent design of the Papists in the Powder Plot; one on the 17th November, in remembrance of that good Queen Elizabeth her entrance unto the Crown; and the third upon the last day of July, in remembrance of the Lord's gracious deliverance from the Spanish Armada in 88.

Sermons commemorating the Gunpowder Plot and the defeat of the Armada were also commissioned by the wills of Luke Jackson, of Nottingham, on 26 January 1630, and Thomas Hayne, of Leicester, in 1640.

Other occasions for which sermons of thanksgiving were requested included the Great Fire of London and the Battle of Trafalgar. Some testators, however, desired sermons to commemorate more personal deliverances. Hercules Clay, a silk mercer, lived in Newark during its siege by the Scots in the Civil War, in 1643. On three consecutive nights he dreamed that the enemy had fired his house, so, interpreting this as a divinely-inspired premonition (even though most of his fellow-citizens must have been afflicted with identical nightmares), Mr Clay and his family abandoned their house, which was destroyed almost immediately by a mortar-bomb. In gratitude, Clay left £100, the interest on which was to be spent annually, half on penny loaves for the poor, half to pay the vicar for a commemorative sermon on 11 March. A similar gesture was made by Sir John Gayer, a seventeenth-century Lord Mayor of London, whose will endowed a sermon to be preached every October in the church of St Katharine Cree, Leadenhall Street, in thanksgiving for his preservation, through prayer, from being eaten by a lion on the coast of Africa.

The most common bequests, however, were for

charitable purposes, and their range knew no bounds. Hordes of generous testators showered the deserving poor (an essential qualification) with every imaginable benefit: bullocks and cows, white and red herrings, bread

To ward off melancholy, the mourners at his funeral were directed to drink a gallon of ale outside the Blue Boar. (See page 51.)

and cheese, milk, beer, and broth. For festive occasions, there were bequests of wine, ale, plum puddings, tobacco, and snuff. If testamentary evidence is to be believed, England must have boasted the best-dressed paupers in the world, even if their required costume was sometimes a trifle idiosyncratic: coats of grey cloth, faced with baize, and green waistcoats lined with green galloon lace were among the gaudy liveries imposed upon the indigent by well-meaning benefactors. Certain bequests betrayed a degree of ignorance about the lifestyle and needs of the poor; in the parish of Eardisland in Herefordshire, a testator made provision for the distribution to hard-up parishioners on Maundy Thursday each year of thirteen bushels of wheat, thirteen red herrings, thirteen pence, thirteen peppercorns, and — thirteen tennis balls!

Provision of dowries was another favourite form of bequest. In 1880, a Neapolitan merchant called Pasquale Favale, who had become a Londoner by adoption, left £750 to the Corporation of London, the interest on which was to provide dowries every year for three poor girls born in London and aged between sixteen and twenty-five. This charity is still dispensed annually. Signor Favale also left £240 to 'the Editor enjoying the greatest repute in any town of Europe', on condition this talented beneficiary should publish his French novel *Zuleite*, his four-act comedy *An English Election*, and his poems, including one on the Last Judgement. Finally, he bequeathed the work of which he was most proud, a tragic opera called *Alzira*, to 'Her Imperial and Royal Majesty of India and of the United Kingdom of Great Britain', in the hope that Queen Victoria would order its performance for the benefit of the London poor.

Christ's Hospital was a popular object of bequests. The will of Peter Symonds, dated 1586, directed that sixty of the younger Bluecoat boys from Christ's Hospital should attend divine service on Good Friday at the church of All Hallows, Lombard Street, in return for which duty each was to be presented with a new penny, a bun, and a packet of raisins. A larger bequest came from the will, dated 9 August 1749, of James St Amand, who left a portrait of his grandfather and namesake to Christ's Hospital, requiring a receipt from its Treasurer and a promise never to part with the painting. On condition that the Hospital cherished his grandfather's portrait, St Amand bequeathed it all his property, to support the Bluecoat children. The picture was to be kept in the Hospital treasury and produced every year at the first general court held after 1 January, and to be shown annually to a representative of the Vice-Chancellor of Oxford. 'But in case a sight of it be refused to the Vice-Chancellor or his Deputy, then I direct that all my bequests given to Christ's Hospital shall immediately cease.' If that happened, the money was to be transferred to Oxford University (this provision cunningly supplying the Vice-Chancellor with an incentive to carry out his annual inspection), and used to increase the salary of the Bodleian librarian to £120 — provided he was a bachelor — the remainder to be spent on books of quality for the library.

There were some bequests which had a strong flavour of personal eccentricity. Sir John Salter, who died in 1605, was, appropriately, a great benefactor of the Worshipful Company of Salters. A condition in his will, however, imposed upon the beadles and servants of the Company the duty of assembling annually, in the first week of October, at St Magnus' Church, London Bridge, armed with staves. Each was then to knock three times upon the testator's tombstone and enquire, 'How do you do, Brother Salter? I hope you are well.'

More than two centuries later, a resident of Dover named Henry Matson had a traumatic experience. While walking on the pier-head, he accidentally dropped his gold-headed cane through one of the 'tree-nail' holes in the planking. He was so vexed by this that in his will, in 1826, he left a sum of money to the Corporation of Dover, the interest from which was to be used each year for stopping-up the holes in the planks on the pier-head. Any surplus was to go towards refreshments for the officers of the Corporation. So the Mayor and Corporation went through the motions, annually, of filling-in a few holes, and then devoted the rest of the money to holding a dinner in a local hotel; at the end of the meal, they would all sign a document certifying that the holes had been duly repaired.

Sometimes it was the testator's chosen method of bestowing largesse which made a will interesting. In the nineteenth century, a prominent American citizen left his widow, yearly, her own weight in gold. This was one woman, therefore, who had no dread of putting on weight; her husband's bequest gave her an average of 1,161 troy ounces of gold every year for the remainder of her life, plus a small additional income from fees paid by members of the public who wished to be present at the weighing ceremony. More originally, a Scots testator who had two young daughters bequeathed a lump sum to each, consisting of her weight in £1 banknotes: the elder, and slimmer, inherited £51,200 by this means, while the younger received £57,344 — the wages, presumably, of puppy-fat!

Generally, however, as in the case of legacies to animals, the quaintness of bequests has derived from the unusual choice of recipient. For example, in 1931, someone left £100 to the editor of *The Times*, for the benefit of his staff, 'in gratitude for the daily pleasure from that paper during a long life'. That was an understandable sentiment; less comprehensible, though, is the notion of the Chancellor of the Exchequer as a deserving object of charity. Nevertheless, Mrs Rose Mary Clarke, of Leicester, whose will was proved in 1961, bequeathed almost a third of her £3,451 estate 'for the Chancellor of the Exchequer in recognition of the provision of a pension which has saved me anxiety and worry during my old age'. Ten years later, and more spectacularly, Miss Marjorie Jesson, of Bournemouth, left £16,000 to the members of her family, and £20,000 to the Chancellor, to assist 'repayment of the national debt'. A close friend said of Miss Jesson: 'She was very patriotic. She thought the country needed the money more than her family.'

There really is no limit to the whimsy of testators in selecting heirs. A Finn once left his entire estate to the Devil, but was posthumously frustrated in his purpose by the courts' refusal to uphold the bequest. A more recent example, however, suggests a resurgence of piety among will-makers. Mr Ernest Digweed, a retired schoolmaster from Portsmouth, died in 1976 at the age of eighty-one. In his will, he ordered that his entire estate of £26,107 was to be invested for eighty years — in trust for a very exalted beneficiary. 'If during those 80 years,' Mr Digweed directed, 'the Lord Jesus Christ shall come to reign on Earth, then the Public Trustee, upon obtaining proof which shall satisfy them of his identity, shall pay to the Lord Jesus Christ all the property which they hold on his behalf.' But Mr Digweed's patience was not inexhaustible; after twenty-one years, the accumulated interest was to go to the Crown, and if Christ had not appeared to claim his inheritance when the eighty years had expired, then the whole estate was likewise to revert to the testator's earthly ruler. This was surely the ultimate gesture: by imposing penalties on the Son of God, Ernest Digweed brought several millennia of testamentary eccentricity to a blasphemous, but logical conclusion.

Codicil

As the preceding chapters have shown, the world of will-making has not become any less contentious since 1544, when Charles Brandon, Duke of Suffolk, the adventurer who had audaciously won the hand of Henry VIII's sister, lamented in his own testament 'the greate ambiguities, doubtes, and questiones that dayly do ryse and growe in last willes . . .' His pessimism was borne out, for he was buried at St George's Chapel, Windsor, in defiance of his own request to be interred at Tattershall.

'The art of will-making,' declared William Hazlitt, who had some pretensions to being an oracle on the subject, 'chiefly consists in baffling the importunity of expectation.' The same point was made, with even more force, if perhaps less felicitous a style, by Sarah Ford, an American testatrix, who wrote in her will: 'i shall give our Clara what i have when i die but she shant have anything until the good Spirit calls me for then she wont get Saucy at me.'

During the last century, the favourite toast among lawyers on the Northern Circuit was 'Country Schoolmasters', since they were foremost among amateur will-makers, and thus great providers of litigation. While it is undoubtedly true that do-it-yourself will-making is fraught with hazards, this supercilious attitude underestimates the ingenuity of laymen who have frequently managed to write perfectly valid wills in the most unpretentious way.

Probably the most homely example is that of Mrs Maggie Nothe, an American housewife, who made her will in her recipe book, as a postscript to the ingredients for 'Chili Sauce Without Working'. The document, as proved in 1913, read: '4 quarts of ripe tomatoes, 4 small onions, 4 green peppers, 2 teacups of sugar, 2 quarts of cider vinegar, 2 ounces ground allspice, 2 ounces cloves, 2 ounces cinnamon, 12 teaspoonfuls salt. Chop tomatoes, onions and peppers fine, add the rest mixed together and bottle cold. Measure tomatoes when peeled. In case I die before my husband I leave everything to him — (signed) MAGGIE NOTHE.'

In contrast to this domestic simplicity, however, a male testator in the same American state waxed lyrical: 'As time rolls on its ceaseless way I find myself gradually losing my grip on life's anchorage, and feel that I must soon drift into that port from which no return tickets are issued. And now dear friends good-bye. P-e-r-h-a-p-s I'll see you later in the sweet Good bye. Sincerely and affectionately Yours J. GILBERT WILLIAMS.'

As already noted, however, many testators are far from charitably disposed when making their last wills and testaments. The examples which have been quoted are the merest tip of the iceberg. While dealing with American wills, it would be remiss not to quote that of Mrs Mary Burns, whose parting tribute to her husband, published in 1907, stated:

> Mr Burns has not ever paid his marriage expenses to his wife. Mr Burns on his way to church had to borrow $5. In days of sickness as well as of health the husband did not bring the least joy to his wife. Wherefore he is a curiosity. He never treated her to anything. She honors him now with $5 as he deserves it.

Since American husbands are henpecked to a degree that has become legendary, it was only to be expected that they would employ their wills as instruments of posthumous revenge. Representative of his oppressed tribe was Daniel Ross, in 1928:

For my tyrranical wife, who did not give me any peace during the last 24 years since I am married to her I leave one dollar for which to buy a rope and hang herself. This is the 4 Will I made in the last 3 years. There was not a married man yet more miserable yet.

But the ultimate broadside of hatred came four years later from Harry Charles Preston. After reluctantly leaving his wife one-third of his estate, as required by local law, he added:

It is my earnest desire and everlasting wish that the above-named adultress and fiend in human form, to whose wiles I fell a victim while temporarily separated from my first wife, this harlot whose insidious lies, poured into my ear daily, caused me to take the step which made a reconciliation with my first wife impossible, this she-devil . . . this unnameable beast, who has made life for me a living hell for the last three years or more, and by whom I stand in daily fear of being murdered while asleep I repeat, it is my everlasting wish that this woman, whom I am compelled by law to call my wife, shall not receive one cent more of my very modest estate than she is entitled to under the laws of the State of Pennsylvania.

These remarks suggest that some of the sparkle had gone out of Mr Preston's marriage. With such vigorous vituperation flourishing in the New World, however, it seems that the future of the malevolent will is secure.

Equally invincible is the tradition of using one's will to express loathing for certain categories of people. To the cases already noted, many others could be added, among them that of William Farren, towards the close of Victoria's reign, whose dread of Cambridge students was extreme. In his will, therefore, he was concerned to arrange the disposition of his estate in a way calculated 'to save my family from keeping or living in an undergraduate lodging-house, as undergraduates are more like wolves and dogs than human beings'.

More recently, a universal phobia was given expression in the will of Mr Edward Horley, a bachelor coal merchant who was also a former Mayor of Altrincham. When he died in 1975 at the age of seventy-six, his will was found to contain instructions to his solicitors to buy a lemon with what was left of his estate after duty, cut it in two, and send one half to the Income Tax inspectorate and the other to the tax collector, with the message: 'Now squeeze this.' Mr Horley's request was carried out, on 15 August 1975.

The coffin, though made of oak, was to be lined with the cedar of his old Havannah cigar boxes. (See page 50.)

Sometimes a will, not in itself eccentric, presented the executors with problems because of bizarre extraneous circumstances. For example, in 1951, a case arose in which an individual who, when the will was made, had been a daughter of the testator, had subsequently changed sex. After his death, a summons was taken out to establish whether the deceased man could be regarded as identical with the female beneficiary mentioned in the will. The judge ruled that there was ample evidence in favour of recognizing him.

At other times, testators found themselves daunted by the responsibility of disposing of their estates. The following advertisement appeared in the personal column of *The Times,* on 29 March 1957: 'Suggestions are invited as to the disposal of about £30,000 for the common good by means of one or more legacies.' Even the normally imperturbable management of that famous newspaper were intrigued by this unusual 'agony' notice, and made enquiries. They were able to inform their readers that the advertiser was an elderly bachelor who had no surviving relatives. 'Everyone must make a will,' he had told *The Times*, 'and I am interested to see what suggestions people will make for the disposal of the money for non-religious purposes. And that is all there is to it.'

Often it is the domestic incongruities among its provisions which lend charm to a will, such as that of Sir Walter Manney, dated at London, St Andrew's Day, 1371, which included bequests 'to my two bastard daughters, nuns, viz. to Mailosel and Malplesant, the one CC franks, the other C franks'. But it was more frequently the extravagant demands made by testators which earned notoriety for their wills. A twentieth-century *cause célèbre* was that of George Bernard Shaw. The contentious clauses in his will, proved on 20 March 1951, were those which provided for setting up an investigation into the possibility of substituting an alphabet of at least forty letters, for the existing one of twenty-six. In particular, he requested that his play *Androcles and the Lion* should be transliterated into the experimental alphabet and printed, page by page, with the conventional text opposite. Six years later, litigation ensued, involving the three bodies interested in the case as residuary legatees — the British Museum, the Royal Academy of Dramatic Art, and the

National Gallery of Ireland.

The case was heard before Mr Justice Harman who himself made several Shavian comments during the hearing. 'Why invent new sounds when there are perfectly good old ones?' he asked at one point, later observing, 'There is another way of spelling 'Shaw' — and that is, by beginning it with a P.' While one of the counsel for the Attorney-General was developing his argument, the learned judge confided to him: 'I think I should disclose to you that a large and heavy tome has arrived in my room. I have not read it, and I propose to hand it down to you. I should not be able to understand it, because it contains square roots and things of that sort.'

There seemed to be a general scepticism regarding philological pedantry among the lawyers present, and, while demolishing the argument that transliteration of *Androcles and the Lion* could be construed as a charitable purpose, counsel for the trustees of the British Museum remarked that he would be interested to see the revised version of the passage 'Did ums get an awful thorn into ums tootsums—wootsums?' Giving judgement, on 20 February 1957, Mr Justice Harman found that the alphabet trusts were invalid and must fail. After a vigorous campaign by the Shaw Society, however, a compromise was arranged at the end of that year, whereby the Public Trustee was to receive sufficient money to carry out the alphabet provisions.

G.B.S. was by no means the most unreasonable testator, as regards provisions for academic research. That honour probably belongs to James Kidd, an Arizona copper-miner who had a genius for playing the stock-market, and who disappeared without trace in 1950. In his will, dated 1946, he directed that his $225,000 estate should go to whoever, individually or collectively, could undertake research, 'or make scientific proof that the soul leaves the body at death'. Probate Judge Robert Myers opened the hearing of claims at Phoenix, Arizona, in March 1967. At that time there were forty applicants, but as the hearing, and consequent publicity, progressed, the number more than doubled.

Among the hopefuls was Mr Russel Dilts, who displayed a photograph of himself with a ghostly face looking over his shoulder; this, he claimed, was the late Mr Kidd. He then went on to explain that he could identify spirits with whom he was in contact 'from the vibrations of their chakras'. Further questioning elicited the fact that 'chakras' were 'the sensitive centres in the departed souls which make contact with humans on earth'.

Even Mr Dilts's soft-centres were eclipsed, however, by the claims of Mrs Jean Bright — appropriately named, since she turned out to be connected 'by a cord of light' to a dentist who had died in 1965. The authority of his dread profession had apparently been sustained beyond the grave, for he acted as spokesman for his fellow departed souls, answering questions put to him by Mrs Bright. She explained that he did this by 'violently contracting the muscles in my abdomen. He contacts me through my nervous system' — a reaction common enough even in intercourse with dentists on this side of eternity. Unhappily, when Mrs Bright demonstrated this relationship in court, elegantly attired in a large electric hairdryer to prevent her receiving messages through her ears instead of her abdomen, her dentist gave wrong answers to many of the questions put to him, including what day it was on earth.

Another odd feature of wills is the unreal nature of some bequests. Cardinal York, the younger brother of Bonnie Prince Charlie, known to his Jacobite followers as Henry IX, died in 1807, when his will, dated 15 July 1802, bequeathed the throne of Great Britain 'to whom the right shall belong by proximity of blood', a gesture of intransigence which fuelled the diehard loyalty of many romantic Jacobites who, to this day, toast the Duke of Bavaria as rightful King of England.

Even more generously, Wilson E. Stoudt, an American testator whose will was proved in 1930, wrote:

> To Mrs Charles L. Stoudt I give and bequeath all that certain Parcel of land From the Atlantic to the Pacific with all the trees and every living thing thereon; and to Charles L. Stoudt, Jr., I give the Four Winds of the Earth that he may Enjoy them the same as I have.

The sordid side of will-making has always involved a degree of trickery. None was more ingenious than the time-honoured Irish custom of placing a live fly in a dead man's mouth while his will was being forged and fraudulently witnessed. The witnesses could then testify under oath that they had seen the will drawn up while the testator 'had life in him', this being a literal translation of the Irish, meaning 'he was alive'.

But such dubious transactions cannot seriously impair the romance that has always surrounded wills. For it does happen, in real life, that people do occasionally benefit from unexpected windfalls which one would think could be found only between the covers of a romantic novel. In 1930, for example, a hairdresser's assistant from Pontypridd was standing in Cardiff station when she was approached by an old lady who explained that she had lost her purse and needed ten shillings for her fare home to Swansea. So the girl lent the old lady ten shillings, which was returned a few days later, with a letter of thanks. The Good Samaritan, no doubt relieved to get her money back, thought no more about it. The following year, however, she was astonished to be contacted by a firm of Swansea solicitors who told her that the old lady had died, leaving her £3,000 as a reward for her kindness. It is stories like that which send us out into the streets, fired with renewed resolution to escort old ladies relentlessly across roads, in the hope of finding ourselves beneficiaries under their wills.

It is worth remembering, too, as further encouragement, that it is never too late to inherit. On 10 December 1976, Mrs Alice White, aged 102, won an action in the

High Court which entitled her to her late sister's £6,000 estate in its entirety, instead of just a life interest. The Court moved to Mrs White's nursing-home at Westcliff-on-Sea, Essex, in order to hear her evidence, which the judge described as 'marvellously clear, incredibly to the point, and very, very impressive'. On the other hand, arguably the most public-spirited will of all time was that of a Mr Stokes, in the nineteenth century: he declared that anyone named as a beneficiary in his will would lose all claim upon his estate if he or she raised any legal action in connection with it.

And what was the most cheerful will? Probably that of Mr Thomas Blyth, a late Victorian testator, who took an obvious pleasure in the arrangements which some of his friends had made for perpetuating his memory. After ordering, sensibly enough, that no one was to wear mourning for him at the expense of his estate, he added: 'But I cannot forget the kindness of the ladies who have promised to wear Dolly Varden garters of black and white as a mark of respect for my memory.' It was a charming memorial, belying the supposedly puritanical character of the Victorians, and certainly an improvement on many of the dispositions made by testators who proclaimed themselves of sound mind!

Selected Sources of Material

H. Edwards, *A Collection of Old English Customs and Curious Bequests and Charities*, London, 1842.

William Tegg, *Wills of their Own, Curious, Eccentric and Benevolent*, London, Wm. Tegg & Co., 1876.

Julia Clara Busk, *Curiosities of the Search-Room*, London, Chapman & Hall Ltd., 1880.

Camden Society Publications, vol LXXXIII, *Wills of Eminent Persons, from Doctors' Commons*.

Croake James, *Curiosities of Law and Lawyers*, 1882.

Notes and Queries, 1849-1940.

The Times, 1930-1976.

Robert Chambers, *Book of Days*, 2 vols, 1864.

Chambers' Journal, vol XIX, 1882.

All The Year Round (Article: 'Wills: Old and New'), 23 August 1890, pp. 178-181.

The English Illustrated Magazine, vol XVII (Article: 'Curious Wills of Curious People', by Charles G. Cutler), 1897, pp. 171-173.

The Strand Magazine, vol XIV (Article: 'Some Peculiar Wills', by L. S. Lewis), 1897, pp. 441-447.